THOMAS HOOD

THOMAS HOOD

Selected Poems

*Edited with an Introduction and Notes
by Joy Flint*

Fyfield Books

To RFF and KF

First published in 1992 by
Carcanet Press Limited
208-212 Corn Exchange Buildings
Manchester M4 3BQ

A CIP catalogue record for this book
is available from the British Library
ISBN 0 85635 957 2

The publisher acknowledges financial assistance from
the Arts Council of Great Britain

Typeset in 10pt Palatino by Bryan Williamson, Darwen
Printed and bound in England by SRP Ltd, Exeter

Contents

---

† Hood included these in his 1827 volume of serious poems *The Plea of the Midsummer Fairies*.

Introduction

Thomas Hood was remembered affectionately by his children:

> While in Germany, he bought a small toy theatre for us, and
> then...drew, painted and cut out the characters and scenery
> for a tragedy (Paul and Virginia), a spectacle (St George and
> the Dragon), and a pantomime. The figures were very clever,
> and the groups and procession capitally arranged – and the
> dragon *was* a dragon!...On high days and holidays this theatre
> used to be brought out and my father used to perform the
> pieces...He used to extemporise the dialogue...His stage
> management, properties, and machinery were capital, and I
> can still remember the agony with which I used to see the
> wreck in Paul and Virginia break up by degrees, and the bodies
> of the lovers washed in over the breakers. In addition to these
> means of evening entertainment he had a magic lantern, for
> which he painted a number of slides, some humorous and
> some pretty ones – a flight of doves and swallows with a hawk,
> and a little cottage in the snow, with a 'practicable' regiment
> marching over a bridge.

There is much in this Victorian scene which is typical of Hood:
domesticity; sociability; fun; skill – of hand and eye and tongue
– fed by a fertile inventiveness and used to delight an audience.
Characteristically, he appears as a versatile entertainer, respon-
sive to shifting moods, to comedy and tragedy, alive to laughter
and to the threat of the hawk and the terror of the dragon.

He was born into the London Book trade: in the heart of the
City of London, in the Poultry, on 23 May 1799, the second son
and third child of Thomas and Elizabeth Hood. His Scottish father
was by this time an established bookseller and publisher, a part-
ner in the firm of Vernor and Hood. His mother, Elizabeth Sands,
came from a well-known family of engravers.

His father's early death, followed by that of his elder brother, left him with a widowed mother and four sisters. The family resources were limited and Hood's formal education came to an end when he was about fourteen and friends found a position for him as a counting-house clerk. He was, however, a voracious reader; in a sonnet he describes how he 'sat upon a lofty stool' and, under an indulgent master, enlivened his book-keeping by writing verses in imitation of the poets he read, succeeding in 'mingling poetic honey with trade wax' – as he was to do throughout his life. His health had always been poor and when he was advised to change his occupation he was apprenticed to his uncle, Robert Sands, to learn engraving; when it continued to cause concern, he was sent for an extended stay to his Scottish relations near Dundee. It would seem that in the two years he was there he continued to work at engraving and to write, sending contributions to local newspapers. He was also writing poetry: passages of a satire on Dundee society and a poem 'The Bandit' with a Byronic hero, survive.

In the autumn of 1817 he returned home, greatly improved in health, to finish his apprenticeship and to practise as an engraver. The whole process of engraving interested him: he invented a device to ease the labour of drawing lines, and left behind both a prose and a verse treatise on the art. At the same time he continued to write for his own amusement, becoming a member of his local literary society. His mother died in the summer of 1821 and he became responsible for the household; his letters reveal that he worked at home and that two of his sisters helped him in the arduous task of preparing the plates. Hood wrote delightful, spontaneous letters and in one written to a Scottish friend he describes his life about this time: 'Perhaps you will ask what I am doing. Why truly I am T. Hood Scripsit et sculpsit – I am engraving and writing prose and Poetry by turns –'. This was to be the pattern of his future life. Few of his engravings survive but one, published in 1825, prompted Lamb to describe him as 'that half-Hogarth'; entitled *The Progress of Cant*, it had a characteristically satirical theme and illustrated a banner-waving procession of what Hood saw as the outstanding hypocrisies of the

8

time. He never abandoned drawing but produced a constant supply of line-drawings and wood-cuts to illustrate his writing until the time of his death; often these have a crude cartoon vitality which highlights the serious intent beneath the comic surface of many of his poems.

Most importantly for his writing, the artist's observant eye and habitual interest in external detail never left him. For from the beginning of 1821 Hood had become more writer than engraver. John Taylor – of Taylor and Hessey, the publishers of Keats – who had once worked for Hood's father, offered him the position of editorial assistant on *The London Magazine*. Hood was full of enthusiasm: 'I dreamt articles, thought articles, wrote articles... The more irksome parts of authorship, such as the correction of the press, were to me labours of love.' From this time onwards he was a professional author, earning his living by writing and editing.

The London Magazine brought this very young man into the heart of the literary scene of the time, into contact with Lamb, who became a close friend, and with the established figures of the Romantic Movement: Wordsworth, Coleridge, Scott, Hazlitt, de Quincey, Clare. Hood has left lively descriptions of them all in his *Literary Reminiscences*. It introduced him also to J.H. Reynolds, Keats's friend and correspondent. In 1825 Hood was to collaborate with Reynolds in a lightly satirical collection of *Odes and Addresses to Great People*; most of these were by Hood and the popularity of the volume helped to establish his reputation as a comic writer. In the same year he married Reynolds's sister Jane, to whom Keats had also written and sent copies of his poems.

Being so closely associated with a circle of the poet's former friends and so soon after his death, it was not surprising that Hood's own early serious poetry was deeply influenced by Keats. There are echoes of Keats's 1820 volume in poems written by Hood as early as 1821: he was the first disciple and known for many years as the last of the Romantics. But it is a misleading description. Even his physical appearance does not fit the popular image of the young Romantic poet, epitomized in Severn's portrait of Keats, book in hand, by the open window. Portraits of Hood as a young man, both actual and verbal, show a different, more typically Victorian figure:

> In outward appearance, Hood conveyed the idea of a clergyman. His figure slight and invariably dressed in black: his face pallid; the complexion delicate, and features regular; his countenance bespeaking sympathy by its sweet expression of melancholy and suffering.

His was, as he described it himself, relishing the thought that appearances might well be deceptive, a 'Methodist face'.

In the *Reminiscences* he recalled listening, as a young man by Lamb's fireside, to Lamb and Wordsworth discussing the 'promissory notes' left behind by the younger poets, Keats and Shelley. Hood himself was one of the few poets of this younger generation to live on into Victoria's reign. Towards the end of his own, not very long, life he gives an account in a letter of another occasion at which he was present – a dinner of the Literary Fund, held in Greenwich to welcome Charles Dickens home from America. These two social engagements pinpoint Hood's place in the chronology of the nineteenth century literary world exactly. Hood was able to count both Lamb and Dickens among his friends and both valued him as a writer and as a man. 'What a fertile genius (and a quiet good soul withal) is Hood...' wrote Lamb in a letter to a friend. And Dickens, when he heard that Hood was dying:

> He...was a man of great power – of prodigious force and genius as a poet – and not generally known, perhaps, by his best credentials. When he was under the pressure of severe misfortune and illness, and I had never seen him, he went far out of his way to praise me; and wrote in the *Athenaeum* a paper on *The Curiosity Shop*; so full of enthusiasm and high appreciation, and so free from any taint of envy or reluctance to acknowledge me as a young man far more fortunate than himself, that I can hardly bear to think of it.

10

Hood's career, therefore, spans the years which saw the Romantic imagination and temper develop into the Victorian. As a result, besides the intrinsic merit of much of his writing, Hood's work, even the hack-work, has an added dimension and interest: he was part of, and absorbed in, a rapidly expanding literary scene, 'an age of literary industry', as he described it, and his writing reflects, sustains, and sometimes influences, changing public taste and concern.

He worked hard to satisfy the demands of the widening market of middle-class readers, constantly meeting deadlines as contributor to and editor of various periodicals and annuals. He produced, often single-handed, supplying both text and illustrations, a series of *Comic Annuals*, providing 'harmless amusement for the Christmas fireside'. In the last few months of his life he had embarked on the first issues of *Hood's Magazine*, which others carried on after his death.

In many ways he was a successful author, much in demand both as editor and contributor and among the best loved writers of his time; but his life, professional and private, was overshadowed by crippling bouts of ill-health and by financial insecurity. He was financially involved with a firm of engravers which failed and, in 1835, in an attempt to economise and clear his debts, he moved abroad with his young family, first to the Rhine, later settling in Antwerp. The self-imposed exile, though it cut his expenses and provided him with copy, proved disastrous to his health. When he returned to England in 1840 he was chronically sick and, increasingly, in pain. Hood died in 1845, on 3 May, a few weeks before his forty-sixth birthday, after a lifetime wholly spent in writing for the literary magazines of the period.

Repeated misfortunes with publishers and booksellers cast some doubt on his business judgment. Again and again he seemed to put his trust in the wrong people, and, when disappointed, was inclined to litigation; he was often the victim of plagiarism; he made a number of impetuous decisions which proved financially disastrous for him – like the one to withdraw from his share in what became the highly profitable *Athenaeum*.

11

These experiences made him a tireless publicist of the injustices suffered by writers in the very volatile conditions then obtaining in the world of books and periodicals. He pleaded eloquently for 'the dignity of the craft' and, in the campaigning years which preceded the Copyright Bill of 1842, for the rights of the author: 'He writes for bread, and gets it short weight; for money and gets the wrong change; for the Present, and he is pirated; for the Future, and his children are disinherited for his pains.' He exerted himself energetically on behalf of individual authors and actors who had fallen on hard times, and in his turn he commanded the loyalty and affectionate regard of his colleagues; many friends rallied to help him through his own difficulties, to petition for a loan for him from the Literary Fund, to help relieve the burden of editorship in his last years and, finally, through the good offices of Peel, to ensure the granting of a civil list pension to his wife.

His output was prodigious – daunting to anyone attempting a selection of his work. He was endlessly inventive and versatile. Amphibian, at home in both prose and verse and in many varieties of each, he ranges in scope from a comic epigram on the death of the giraffe at the London Zoo to a three-volume novel *Tylney Hall*. He reviewed exhibitions, plays and books – from the newest novels to cookery books and the first *Kelly's Directory*. He wrote sketches and pantomimes for the stage. He wrote travelogues, tales and legends, and humorous snatches of patter and dialogue – radio scripts before their time.

Much of Hood's verse was comic and humorous: he wrote comic ballads; he wrote topical light verse and stronger satire; he wrote children's verses full of a robust playground cruelty, in which animals do not escape the butcher's knife,

> And Ogres draw their cruel knives,
> To shed the blood of girls and boys.

He wrote nonsense verses which can sound – as many of his comic illustrations look – like those of Edward Lear:

12

> *Krak kraziboo ban,*
> I'm the Lunatick Man
> Confined in the Moon since creation began –
> *Sit muggy bigog,*
> Whom except in a fog
> You see with a Lanthorn, a Bush, and a Dog.

In *Miss Kilmansegg and her Precious Leg* he wrote a bizarre, comic, harshly satirical poem in serial form. But he also wrote more conventional serious verse: street ballads, song lyrics and sentimental ballads; traditional sonnets; dramatic monologues; mythological narratives; and a handful of tender, controlled poems, some of which are among the best known in the language. He also wrote poems of social protest which touched the conscience of the nation.

All Hood's poetry should be seen in the context of its production. Most of the poems, even the most intimate, first appeared in popular periodicals; many were written expressly for them and with a specific audience of middle-class readers in mind. Many were written to meet a deadline or fill a vacant space with little time for revision or refinement. Yet even the most recognisably derivative work always bears some mark of originality and there is a competence about even the most obvious hack-work, of which there is plenty; there is no call to doubt his own assertion that he never wrote anything that did not please himself. This professional, working, journalistic background makes him a different kind of poet from most of his Romantic contemporaries. He was no less talented: he was perhaps in many ways more original and technically more gifted, with a facility and virtuosity that earned Auden's admiration, but his sense of poetic vocation was less exalted, less dedicated, less single-minded than theirs. Temperament and circumstances made his view more modest and more commercial but, for all his relentless clowning, he was a serious poet.

When the authorship of the anonymously published *Odes and Addresses to Great People* became known – the quality of the puns

13

caused Coleridge to attribute the volume to Lamb – Hood was quickly established in the minds of the public as a talented writer of comic verse and in his own lifetime it was as a humorist that he was best known, celebrated for his – to modern taste – deplorable puns. He became, as he said, 'lively Hood for a livelihood' and seems to have accepted his role as verbal clown philosophically: 'To make laugh is my calling. I must jump, I must tumble, I must turn language head over heels, and leap through grammar.' He saw his role principally as an entertainer, himself as the literary equivalent of Joseph Grimaldi, that favourite clown, whose portrait hung, alongside that of Lamb, on his study wall.

By all accounts Hood's punning appears to have been instinctive and compulsive and he defends its use: 'having taken out a certificate to "shoot folly as it flies" I shall persist in using the double barrel as long as meanings will rise in coveys'; he insisted that 'A double meaning shows a double sense'. Nor is it 'altogether fool'; Hood is often, like King Lear's companion, 'a bitter fool' and his double meanings reflect on his principal theme, or, as in his play on 'twit' in 'The Song of the Shirt', cast a nervous sidelong glance at life's cruel practical jokes. The most brutal word-play in the ballads – in 'A Waterloo Ballad', for instance – has all the pungency of the parodies current in the trenches of the First World War:

> Alas! a splinter of a shell
> Right in my stomach sticks;
> French mortars don't agree so well
> With stomachs as French bricks.
>
> This very night a merry dance
> At Brussels was to be;–
> Instead of opening a ball,
> A ball has open'd me.

Hood the clown and Hood the serious poet were closer kin than is sometimes supposed. His work lacks the sustained fusion of the sinister and the laughable which characterizes Dickens's

14

mature work but it is Dickens's crowded, kaleidoscopic imagination, that Hood's own, with its dark and comic side, most nearly resembles. Even as a person he often has the air of a character from Dickens; something of Wemmick's split personality dwells in him: the man of sober appearance, fascinated by crime and murder, as excited as his young son when, in Edinburgh they 'saw the shop where the rope was bought to hang Porteous', can switch abruptly into the whimsical host firing a miniature cannon across the lake to welcome friends to his home at Lake House, Wanstead. His patience in adversity recalls Tom Pinch; it is not surprising to find him pleading with Dickens as the parts of *Martin Chuzzlewit* appeared, to 'make Tom Pinch turn author, and Pecksniff become a publisher...'.

Like Dickens and like Lamb he was a Londoner. His many pages of prose and verse are crowded with the life and sounds, people and miscellaneous personalities of London. Shops, theatres, pleasure gardens, Lord Mayor's Show, day trippers on the Thames, rogues, Members of Parliament, are all here. The author of Waverley, 'The Great Unknown', jostles alongside Madame Hengler, firework-maker to Vauxhall and the prison-reformer, Elizabeth Fry accompanies the theatre's most famous clown, Grimaldi; Mr Graham, the Aeronaut, looks down from his balloon on the capital's 'mob of little men... Like mites upon a cheese!'

It was not only the multi-faceted surface of contemporary life to which Hood was alert and sensitive. He was profoundly conscious of deeper undercurrents of change affecting the times in which he lived and quickly aware of the implications for ordinary people of the great technical and industrial advances of the century. He might write in comic vein of the plight of washerwomen in his 'Address to The Steam-Washing Company' or imagine the thoughts of an Under-ostler on the coming of steam, but his concern was serious. Social awareness is obvious enough under the bantering tone and, no doubt irresistible, puns of his 'Friendly Epistle to Mrs Fry', urging her to teach the children of the prisoners outside the walls of the gaol:

15

Come out of Newgate, Mrs Fry! Repair
  Abroad, and find your pupils in the streets,
O, come abroad into the wholesome air,
  And take your moral place, before Sin seats
Her wicked self in the Professor's chair.
  Suppose some morals raw! the true receipt's
To dress them in the pan, but do not try
To cook them in the fire, good Mrs Fry!

But the voice of compassion and social conscience, the voice of the forerunner of Dickens, had been present in Hood's very earliest contribution to *The London Magazine*, which described, in the manner of Sterne, a walk from Islington to Waterloo Bridge, and it rings true: 'I hate the weeping-willow set, who will cry over their pug dogs and canaries, till they have no tears to spare for the real children of misfortune and misery.'

In 1826 and 1827 Hood published two collections of his pieces, in prose and verse, taken from periodicals, under the title *Whims and Oddities*. They contained a motley selection, largely popular ballads and lyrics. In 1827 also he made a collection of his more serious poems under the title *The Plea of the Midsummer Fairies*. The volume was not well received by the public and sales were poor; to the regret of his friends, who valued it more highly, Hood never attempted a similar collection. His reputation as a comic writer was by then so firmly established that when, in 1828, he issued a serious collection of *National Tales*, he felt it necessary to offer an explanation:

Because I have jested elsewhere, it does not follow that I am incompetent for gravity . . . It is from none of the player's ambition, which has led the buffoon by a rash step to the tragic buskin, that I assume the sadder humour, but because I know from certain passages that such affections are not foreign to my nature. During my short lifetime, I have often been as 'sad as night', and not like the young gentlemen of France, 'merely from wantonness'. It is the contrast of such leaden and golden fits that lends a double relish to our days.

Chronic ill-health ensured that the double vision was always with him and the sadder humour often cast its shadow. An atmosphere of death and foreboding clings to much of Hood's writing, comic as well as serious. In the course of his career it takes many forms: a dream of water babies in 'The Sea of Death',

> And there were spring-faced cherubs that did sleep
> Like water-lilies on that motionless deep,
> How beautiful! with bright unruffled hair
> On sleek unfretted brows...;

or the sub-aqueous light of *Hero and Leander*; or the intrusion of physical cruelty, even in his comic verses for children; or the reflective mood of personal sadness, as in 'I remember, I remember'; his fascination with murder and guilt; his concern for the suicides of Waterloo Bridge; or morbid attraction to the 'narrow house and dark' in 'The Elm Tree'; or saturation in an atmosphere of fear and foreboding in 'The Haunted House'.

It is from the poems in *The Plea of the Midsummer Fairies* that Hood has been most commonly represented in standard anthologies and which are largely responsible for his reputation as a Romantic poet. The influence of Keats is apparent even in many of the titles: 'The Departure of Summer'; 'Ode: to Autumn'; 'To Fancy'; 'Ode to Melancholy'. There are others which are familiar to many readers: the song lyric, 'Fair Ines'; 'Ruth'; the sonnet, 'Silence'; 'I remember, I remember'.

Nearly all the longer narrative poems in the volume have, like those of Keats, a basis in myth and legend: *The Plea of the Midsummer Fairies* itself; *Hero and Leander*; *Lycus, the Centaur*; *The Two Peacocks of Bedfont*. All four of the myths are Hood's inventions. The title poem – dedicated to Lamb – is an elaborate allegory in which the figure of Shakespeare rescues the Midsummer Fairies from the scythe of Time; the Leander of Hood's poem is lured to his death by the sea-nymph, Scylla; *The Two Peacocks of Bedfont* – clipped in yew – is a homespun myth preaching a homily on the wages of Vanity and Pride. *Lycus, the Centaur* is often considered wholly imitative; it certainly owes debts to Keats, to Milton, perhaps to Mary Shelley, but there is some justification for Hartley Coleridge's view that it is a work 'absolutely unique in its line' for the poem is original in several ways. Hood creates a myth to explain the origin of the Centaur, imagining the human Lycus, as victim of a Circean spell which is interrupted before the transformation is complete so that he remains half horse, half man – a Centaur. It is written as an interior monologue. Elsewhere, in his comic poems, with his adroit handling of the vernacular, Hood's use of the monologue looks forward to Browning, sometimes to Kipling; here he anticipates Tennyson. There are passages in this over-long poem, when, contemplating the plight of the beasts under Circe's spell, or Lycus's involuntary exclusion from domestic affection, Hood jars on nerves which Tennyson was to touch in 'Maud' or in 'Lucretius'.

Lycus is written in anapaests: an insensitive choice to many, but the galloping metre seems symptomatic of that nervous instinct which constantly drives Hood into black humour and brutal pun in the face of the unbearable. This is the case with another early poem, printed in *Whims and Oddities* in 1826, on a popular theme of the time, 'The Last Man'. In its use of monologue and its emotional base it resembles *Lycus* but the style, texture and treatment could hardly be more different: 'The Last Man' has all the crude vitality and pace of a street ballad, in which the anti-climax of the stark pun in the final line does not seem out of place.

It was inevitable that as a very young man Hood should have been seduced by Keats's style but 'The Last Man' indicates the much deeper underlying influence, in both manner and substance, that had been exerted by *The Lyrical Ballads* of Wordsworth and Coleridge. It seems fitting that Hood should have been born at the turn of the century when Wordsworth was forming and articulating the perceptions of profound social change and social need which had given rise to *The Lyrical Ballads*. Nearly all of Hood's work, comic and serious, is firmly anchored in a deep conviction of the worth of 'the great and simple affections of our nature' and in his sense of his own common humanity. Even in so apparently Keatsian a poem as 'Ruth', Hood does not emphasize her grief, but, looking through the eyes of Boaz, records the compassionate impulse of the human heart:

> Sure, I said, heav'n did not mean,
> Where I reap thou shouldst but glean,
> Lay thy sheaf adown and come,
> Share my harvest and my home.

With hindsight it is not difficult to discern signs in Hood's early poems of an awakened humanitarian strain which was to strengthen as the century advanced and come to dominate his later poetry.

Coleridge's voice is clearly heard in the stanzas of 'The Last Man':

> My conscience began to gnaw my heart,
> Before the day was done,
> For other men's lives had all gone out,
> Like candles in the sun! –
> But it seem'd as if I had broke, at last,
> A thousand necks in one!

His influence is also strong in a poem first published in 1829, 'The Dream of Eugene Aram'. Like 'The Ancient Mariner' the poem is a study in guilt and remorse but takes as its subject, not an imaginary, but a real crime and an actual criminal. More and more Hood's subject-matter was taken from 'incidents and situations from common life' and his writing, humorous and serious, related to the actual world in which he lived. He consciously turned away from legend, recognizing the inappropriateness of Gothic Romanticism in a rapidly industrialized world. He preferred caricature to what he called 'enthusimoosy' when he came to write the travel sketches in *Up the Rhine*, saying that modern steamboats associated awkwardly with feudal ruins and there had been 'enough of vapouring, in more senses than one, on the blue and castled river.'

His comic poetry had begun to address social and moral evils in a more openly satirical and serious way than the teasing, bantering tone adopted towards topical personalities in the *Odes and Addresses*. In 1837, stung by an unwarranted and personal attack, condemning the 'profaneness and ribaldry' of his work, he used a sharper voice to defend himself and to launch a general attack on hypocrisy and cant in his 'Ode to Rae Wilson'. The poem contains Hood's clearest statement of his philosophy of life:

> Well! – be the graceless lineaments confest!
> I do enjoy this bounteous beauteous earth;
>   And dote upon a jest
> 'Within the limits of becoming mirth'; –
> No solemn sanctimonious face I pull,
> Nor think I'm pious when I'm only bilious –
> Nor study in my sanctum supercilious
> To frame a Sabbath Bill or forge a Bull.
> I pray for grace – repent each sinful act –
> Peruse, but underneath the rose, my Bible;
> And love my neighbour, far too well, in fact,
> To call and twit him with a godly tract
> That's turn'd by application to a libel.
> My heart ferments not with the bigot's leaven,
> All creeds I view with toleration thorough,
> And have a horror of regarding heaven
>   As anybody's rotten borough.

In September 1840 the *New Monthly Magazine* began serialisation of Hood's most grotesque poetic production, *Miss Kilmansegg and her Precious Leg*; it continued to appear in monthly parts until the middle of 1841. This 'golden legend' had as its target the increasing materialism and acquisitiveness of the society he found around him on his return from the continent. The energetic buffoonery is typical of Hood's comic verse but the frenetic pace of its verbal and comic invention – manic punning and accumulation of detail – sustained for so long on a single theme, betray a very serious moral purpose and social message: the 'Methodist face' was not wholly deceptive. Both target and accumulative method in *Miss Kilmansegg* anticipate Dickens's portrayal of the Veneerings in *Our Mutual Friend*.

The humanitarian strain always present in Hood's writing – early in his career he spoke out against slavery – became more pronounced as the century advanced; in the last few years of his life he pleaded directly for the poor and unfortunate victims of the affluent Victorian society he had attacked in *Miss Kilmansegg*. 'The Song of the Shirt' and 'The Pauper's Christmas Carol' reminded well-fed Christmas readers of *Punch* in 1843 of the sweated labour of the seamstresses who produced their finery and of the plight of those in the hated workhouses. Hood was always sympathetic to the hardship and injustice suffered by many women in his society; most poignantly, with a tenderness similar to that which he brought to personal sorrow in 'We watch'd her breathing through the night', he wrote in 'The Bridge of Sighs' of the many suicides who fell to their deaths from Waterloo Bridge.

These poems of social protest were widely circulated and widely influential, voicing and stimulating the awakening moral conscience of the middle classes. Readers in the earlier half of the twentieth century, considering the poems out of their immediate context and forgetting their urgent didactic purpose, found them over-sentimental. But Hood was in tune with the mood of his public: most of the poems were written in response to reports in daily newspapers which had touched his own heart and common humanity. The extent to which he felt for and with these unknown strangers can be gauged from his response to the case of Gifford White, an eighteen-year-old agricultural labourer, desperate for work, who had been sentenced to transportation for life for threatening – no more – to set fire to local farms. The case preyed on Hood's mind in his final illness; he petitioned Members of Parliament on White's behalf and he wrote 'The Lay of the Labourer', haunted, as he said, by the phantom 'of a real person, a living breathing man, with a known name...'.

It is typical of Hood that when he pleads for life's anonymous unfortunates, he thinks of the individual personality, of the 'living breathing man, with a known name'. A single seamstress sings the Song of the Shirt; 'Every soul,' crowding 'in a very torrent of Man' in time to 'The Workhouse Clock', is as distinct as a Lowry figure; the homeless, nameless suicide, lifted up so tenderly from the Thames is 'one more Unfortunate' in a drab world but Hood asserts her individuality with striking economy of detail:

> Loop up her tresses
> Escaped from the comb,
> Her fair auburn tresses;

His instinct to focus on the suffering of a particular individual had always been strong: in his early work it led him to voice the anguish of Lycus and, writing of guilt and remorse, to tell the story, not of any strange and emblematic Ancient Mariner but of an actual criminal 'with a known name' – Eugene Aram, executed in 1759 for a real crime of murder.

What moves Hood most throughout his career is the thought of those men and women cut off from the sympathy and love of their fellow creatures, deprived of domestic affection, by their own actions, by circumstance, or by economic necessity and man's inhumanity to man. He was devoted to his own wife and children, a daughter and a son; his domestic life, in spite of the loss in infancy of their first child – the subject of Lamb's poem 'On an Infant dying as soon as born ' – in spite of precarious finances and his own and Jane's ill-health, was a happy one. 'I feel strongly that my domestic happiness has kept me so long alive', he wrote in a letter in 1843. Elsewhere he noted with regret that there were few examples of 'domestic poetry' in English, as there were in Scottish, poetry. When he expresses personal emotion directly in his poetry it is of these intimate domestic feelings that he writes: of his love for his wife and children, or of the memories or deaths of those he loved. Here he is self-effacing, unassuming, unsentimental; these poems, sparse, tender and restrained, carry with them the assurance that Hood's more demonstrative cries on behalf of the poor and oppressed are founded securely on genuine feeling and understanding.

Hood's darkest poetry springs from his dread of losing all that is essentially dear to him. 'The Haunted House' is a nightmare projection of this blankness, 'where Love, domestic Love, no longer nestles':

> A residence for woman, child, and man,
> A dwelling-place – and yet no habitation;
> A House, – but under some prodigious ban
> Of excommunication.

The vision of blank desertion, of a complete absence of life and affection had recurred throughout his life: it is there in the fragment 'The Sea of Death'; or in the sonnet 'Silence'; it is the horror felt by 'The Last Man', by Lycus and by Eugene Aram, the void sensed at the heart of *Miss Kilmansegg*. The compassion which informs all his writing – even the blackest humour of the stinging puns – springs from an anguished apprehension of a life severed from domestic care and love. It prompts him to plead directly to the general reading public in 'The Bridge of Sighs':

> Touch her not scornfully
> Think of her mournfully,
> Gently and humanly;

and to reflect, in that supposedly moral Victorian society:

> Alas! for the rarity
> Of Christian charity
> Under the sun!
> Oh! it was pitiful!
> Near a whole city full,
> Home she had none!

Hood wrote for a living, to please a public and to pay his debts and therefore his estimate of his role as poet was a modest one but he never lost sight of 'the dignity of the craft' and its moral obligations. At the lowest level, in his *Comic Annuals*, by 'humbly contributing to the greatest entertainment of the greatest number', he hoped 'to be of use' to his countrymen; it was a matter of pride to him that, in spite of his addiction to the double meaning, 'the reproach of impurity has never been cast upon me by my judges'. As entertainer his aim was to spread 'a cheerful philosophy', to foster the domestic virtues and at the same time, as he did fearlessly throughout his career, to expose hypocrisy wherever he found it and to alert the conscience of society to the plight of the poor in their midst. He never failed, as he wrote of Dickens, to remind 'wealth of the claims of want, the feasting of the fasting'.

It was not surprising that Hood should have been quick to identify the young Dickens as a kindred spirit and to realize that the Romantic humanitarian impetus had begun to find a new channel of literary expression in the novel. Writing of Boz in 1839 he recognized that 'his drift is a natural one: along with the great human currents and not against them'. Much in Hood anticipates the social concern and moral stance of the mid-century reforming novelists: Dickens, Eliot and Gaskell. The diversity and scope of his work, its wide distribution and popularity, demonstrates very clearly both the continuity of the Romantic tradition and the way in which those ideas and sensibilities filtered through into popular literature, pervading and influencing the consciousness of an avid and widening, predominantly urban, reading public.

Reviewing Hood's total output, appreciating his technical virtuosity, openness to new influences and willingness to experiment, his keen awareness of social and cultural change, acknowledging also the imaginative power and independent achievement of some of his poems, it is tempting to think that he had been constrained by illness and poverty to waste his talents. Many of his contemporaries thought so, Thackeray among them:

> Here is a man with a power to touch the heart almost unequalled, and he passes days and years in writing, "Young Ben he was a nice young man," and so forth ... "You great man, you good man, you true genius and poet," I cry out, as I turn page after page. "Do, do, make no more of these jokes, but be yourself, and take your station."

Hood knew himself better; it is unlikely that he would have

agreed. His was essentially a quicksilver temperament, thoughtful but not contemplative, diverted and fascinated by every aspect of life, trivial or grave, restlessly finding outlet and expression in many different forms.

One of the incidental pleasures of reading widely in Hood's work is the frequency with which the ear catches tones and cadences, not merely echoes of past voices, but anticipations also of many differing writers who came after him. Most modern readers know Hood only from anthologies – a few of the shorter serious poems, or one of his light verses, or a poem of social protest. He is a much more coherent poet than reading him in this piecemeal fashion suggests. All that he writes springs from delight in and concern for his fellow creatures, whether he wishes to move them to laughter, to tears, or to action; he commands both affection and respect.

At heart Hood is a serious and moral poet – the shadow of the hawk always darkened his sky, the dragon *was* a dragon – but he never forgot the value of pantomime, toy theatre and magic lantern, recognizing the need for fantasy in the face of harsh reality. Like his own Lycus he remains a hybrid creature: half-clown, half-preacher; light-hearted but gravely haunted; Romantic and Victorian; terse one moment, garrulous the next; illustrator, journalist, and poet.

Note

This short selection aims to represent the range, diversity, and continuity of Hood's poetry. Inevitably selection from such a prolific writer has meant the exclusion of much that is interesting or attractive and only token representation of some of the longer poems.

The publication history of Hood's poems is complex. Periodicals and Annuals proliferated throughout the nineteenth century and Hood was connected with, and contributed to many of them. He was on the staff of *The London Magazine* from 1821-23; was one of the group which ran *The Athenaeum* in 1829; edited the first volume of *The Gem*, 1829; he produced a series of *Comic Annuals* from 1830-39, another in 1842 – and some of their contents were re-issued in monthly parts under the title *Hood's Own*; he edited *The New Monthly Magazine* from 1841-43; edited his own publication *Hood's Magazine* from 1844-45, which continued after his death. He contributed also to some of the many keepsake volumes which were produced in this period, such as *Friendship's Offering*, and Ackermann's *Forget-me-Not*. Hood also made collections, largely consisting of his contributions to periodicals and issued them in volume form: *Whims and Oddities*, 1826 and 1827; *The Plea of the Midsummer Fairies*, 1827; *Whimsicalities*, 1844.

As far as possible the poems are arranged chronologically, according to their first known publication date, although the version printed incorporates any later revisions.

To Hope
lines 43-62

... Alas! alas!
How pleasures pass,
And leave thee now no subject, save
The peace and bliss beyond the grave!

Then be thy flight among the skies;
Take, then, Oh! take the skylark's wing,
And leave dull earth, and heav'nward rise
O'er all its tearful clouds, and sing
　On skylark's wing!

Another life-spring there adorns
Another youth, – without the dread
Of cruel care, whose crown of thorns
Is here for manhood's aching head. –
Oh, there are realms of welcome day,
A world where tears are wiped away!
Then be thy flight among the skies;
Take then, Oh! take the skylark's wing,
And leave dull earth, and heav'nward rise
O'er all its tearful clouds, and sing
　On skylark's wing!

The London Magazine, 1821

The Sea of Death
A fragment

　　　– Methought I saw
Life swiftly treading over endless space;
And, at her foot-print, but a bygone pace,
The ocean-past, which, with increasing wave,
Swallow'd her steps like a pursuing grave.

Sad were my thoughts that anchor'd silently
On the dead waters of that passionless sea,
Unstirr'd by any touch of living breath:
Silence hung over it, and drowsy Death,
Like a gorged sea-bird, slept with folded wings
On crowded carcases – sad passive things
That wore the thin grey surface, like a veil
Over the calmness of their features pale.

And there were spring-faced cherubs that did sleep
Like water-lilies on that motionless deep,
How beautiful! with bright unruffled hair
On sleek unfretted brows, and eyes that were
Buried in marble tombs, a pale eclipse!
And smile-bedimpled cheeks, and pleasant lips,
Meekly apart, as if the soul intense
Spake out in dreams of its own innocence:
And so they lay in loveliness, and kept
The birth-night of their peace, that Life e'en wept
With very envy of their happy fronts;
For there were neighbour brows scarr'd by the brunts
Of strife and sorrowing – where Care had set
His crooked autograph, and marr'd the jet
Of glossy locks, with hollow eyes forlorn,
And lips that curl'd in bitterness and scorn –
Wretched, – as they had breathed of this world's pain,
And so bequeath'd it to the world again
Through the beholder's heart in heavy sighs.

So lay they garmented in torpid light,
Under the pall of a transparent night,
Like solemn apparitions lull'd sublime
To everlasting rest, – and with them Time
Slept, as he sleeps upon the silent face
Of a dark dial in a sunless place.

The London Magazine, 1822

Faithless Sally Brown
An Old Ballad

Young Ben he was a nice young man,
  A carpenter by trade;
And he fell in love with Sally Brown,
  That was a lady's maid.

But as they fetch'd a walk one day,
  They met a press-gang crew;
And Sally she did faint away,
  Whilst Ben he was brought to.

The Boatswain swore with wicked words,
  Enough to shock a saint,
That though she did seem in a fit,
  'Twas nothing but a feint.

'Come, girl,' said he, 'hold up your head,'
  He'll be as good as me;
For when your swain is in our boat,
  A boatswain he will be.'

So when they'd made their game of her,
  And taken off her elf,
She roused, and found she only was
  A coming to herself.

'And is he gone, and is he gone?'
  She cried and wept outright:
'Then I will to the water side,
  And see him out of sight.'

A waterman came up to her, –
  'Now, young woman,' said he,
'If you weep on so, you will make
  Eye-water in the sea.'

'Alas! they've taken my beau Ben
    To sail with old Benbow;'
And her woe began to run afresh,
    As if she'd said Gee woe!

Says he, 'They've only taken him
    To the Tender ship, you see;'
'The Tender-ship,' cried Sally Brown,
    'What a hard-ship that must be!'

'O! would I were a mermaid now,
    For then I'd follow him;
But Oh! – I'm not a fish-woman,
    And so I cannot swim.

'Alas! I was not born beneath
    The virgin and the scales,
So I must curse my cruel stars,
    And walk about in Wales.'

Now Ben had sail'd to many a place
    That's underneath the world;
But in two years the ship came home,
    And all her sails were furl'd.

But when he call'd on Sally Brown,
    To see how she went on,
He found she'd got another Ben,
    Whose Christian name was John.

'O Sally Brown, O Sally Brown,
    How could you serve me so?
I've met with many a breeze before,
    But never such a blow:'

Then reading on his 'bacco box
   He heav'd a bitter sigh,
And then began to eye his pipe,
   And then to pipe his eye.

And then he tried to sing 'All's Well,'
   But could not though he tried;
His head was turn'd, and so he chew'd
   His pigtail till he died.

His death, which happen'd in his berth,
   At forty-odd befell:
They went and told the sexton, and
   The sexton toll'd the bell.

The London Magazine, 1822

Lycus, the Centaur
lines 23-71

'Lycus, detained by Circe' wanders in human form
'in her magical dominion':

And I pluck'd of the fruit with held breath, and a fear
That the branch would start back and scream out in my ear;
For once, at my suppering, I pluck'd in the dusk
An apple, juice-gushing and fragrant of musk;
But by daylight my fingers were crimson'd with gore,
And the half-eaten fragment was flesh at the core;
And once – only once – for the love of its blush,
I broke a bloom bough, but there came such a gush
On my hand, that it fainted away in weak fright,
While the leaf-hidden woodpecker shriek'd at the sight;

And oh! such an agony thrill'd in that note,
That my soul, startling up, beat its wings in my throat,
As it long'd to be free of a body whose hand
Was doom'd to work torments a Fury had plann'd!

There I stood without stir, yet how willing to flee,
As if rooted and horror-turn'd into a tree, –
Oh! for innocent death, – and to suddenly win it,
I drank of the stream, but no poison was in it;
I plung'd in its waters, but ere I could sink,
Some invisible fate pull'd me back to the brink;
I sprang from the rock, from its pinnacle height,
But fell on the grass with a grasshopper's flight;
I ran at my fears – they were fears and no more,
For the bear would not mangle my limbs, nor the boar,
But moan'd, – all their brutaliz'd flesh could not smother,
The horrible truth, – we were kin to each other!

They were mournfully gentle, and group'd for relief,
All foes in their skin, but all friends in their grief:
The leopard was there, – baby-mild in its feature;
And the tiger, black barr'd, with the gaze of a creature
That knew gentle pity; the bristle-back'd boar,
His innocent tusks stain'd with mulberry gore;
And the laughing hyena – but laughing no more;
And the snake, not with magical orbs to devise
Strange death, but with woman's attraction of eyes;
The tall ugly ape, that still bore a dim shine
Through his hairy eclipse of a manhood divine;
And the elephant stately, with more than its reason,
How thoughtful in sadness! but this is no season
To reckon them up from the lag-bellied toad
To the mammoth, whose sobs shook his ponderous load.
There were woes of all shapes, wretched forms, when I came,
That hung down their heads with a human-like shame;
The elephant hid in the boughs, and the bear

Shed over his eyes the dark veil of his hair;
And the womanly soul turning sick with disgust,
Tried to vomit herself from her serpentine crust;
While all groan'd their groans into one at their lot,
As I brought them the image of what they were not.

lines 350-424

*Lycus is beloved by a Water Nymph to whom Circe gives an incantation
to pronounce which will turn him into a horse and render him immortal;
appalled by the horrible effect of the charm, she breaks off in the middle,
and he becomes a Centaur – half man, half horse.*

             ... Then I ask'd of the wave,
What monster I was, and it trembled and gave
The true shape of my grief, and I turn'd with my face
From all waters for ever, and fled through that place,
Till with horror more strong than all magic I pass'd
Its bounds, and the world was before me at last.

   There I wander'd in sorrow, and shunn'd the abodes
Of men, that stood up in the likeness of Gods,
But I saw from afar the warm shine of the sun
On their cities, where man was a million, not one;
And I saw the white smoke of their altars ascending,
That show'd where the hearts of the many were blending,
And the wind in my face brought shrill voices that came
From the trumpets that gather'd whole bands in one fame
As a chorus of man, – and they stream'd from the gates
Like a dusky libation pour'd out to the Fates.
But at times there were gentler processions of peace
That I watch'd with my soul in my eyes till their cease,
There were women! there men! but to me a third sex
I saw them all dots – yet I loved them as specks:
And oft to assuage a sad yearning of eyes

I stole near the city, but stole covert-wise
Like a wild beast of love, and perchance to be smitten
By some hand that I rather had wept on than bitten!
Oh, I once had a haunt near a cot where a mother
Daily sat in the shade with her child, and would smother
Its eyelids in kisses, and then in its sleep
Sang dreams in its ear of its manhood, while deep
In a thicket of willows I gazed o'er the brooks
That murmur'd between us and kiss'd them with looks;
But the willows unbosom'd their secret, and never
I return'd to a spot I had startled for ever,
Though I oft long'd to know, but could ask it of none,
Was the mother still fair, and how big was her son?

For the haunters of fields they all shunn'd me by flight,
The men in their horror, the women in fright;
None ever remain'd save a child once that sported
Among the wild bluebells, and playfully courted
The breeze; and beside him a speckled snake lay
Tight strangled, because it had hiss'd him away
From the flow'r at his finger; he rose and drew near
Like a Son of Immortals, one born to no fear,
But with strength of black locks and with eyes azure bright
To grow to large manhood of merciful might.
He came, with his face of bold wonder, to feel
The hair of my side, and to lift up my heel,
And question'd my face with wide eyes; but when under
My lids he saw tears, – for I wept at his wonder,
He stroked me, and utter'd such kindliness then,
That the once love of women, the friendship of men
In past sorrow, no kindness e'er came like a kiss
On my heart in its desolate day such as this!
And I yearn'd at his cheeks in my love, and down bent,
And lifted him up in my arms with intent
To kiss him, – but he cruel-kindly, alas!
Held out to my lips a pluck'd handful of grass!

34

Then I dropt him in horror, but felt as I fled
The stone he indignantly hurl'd at my head,
That dissever'd my ear, – but I felt not, whose fate
Was to meet more distress in his love than his hate!

Thus I wander'd, companion'd of grief and forlorn,
Till I wish'd for that land where my being was born,
But what was that land with its love, where my home
Was self-shut against me; for why should I come
Like an after-distress to my grey-bearded father,
With a blight to the last of his sight? – let him rather
Lament me for dead, and shed tears in the urn
Where I was not, and still in fond memory turn
To his son even such as he left him. Oh, how
Could I walk with the youth once my fellows, but now
Like Gods to my humble estate? – or how bear
The steeds once the pride of my eyes and the care
Of my hands? Then I turn'd me self-banish'd, and came
Into Thessaly here, where I met with the same
As myself.

The London Magazine, 1822

Sonnet: To Fancy

Most delicate Ariel! submissive thing,
Won by the mind's high magic to its hest, –
Invisible embassy, or secret guest, –
Weighing the light air on a lighter wing; –
Whether into the midnight moon, to bring
Illuminate visions to the eye of rest, –
Or rich romances from the florid West, –
Or to the sea, for mystic whispering, –

35

Still by thy charm'd allegiance to the will,
The fruitful wishes prosper in the brain,
As by the fingering of fairy skill, –
Moonlight, and waters, and soft music's strain,
Odours, and blooms, and *my* Miranda's smile,
Making this dull world an enchanted isle.

The London Magazine, 1822

Fair Ines

O saw ye not fair Ines?
She's gone into the West,
To dazzle when the sun is down,
And rob the world of rest:
She took our daylight with her,
The smiles that we love best,
With morning blushes on her cheek,
And pearls upon her breast.

O turn again, fair Ines,
Before the fall of night,
For fear the Moon should shine alone,
And stars unrivall'd bright;
And blessed will the lover be
That walks beneath their light,
And breathes the love against thy cheek
I dare not even write!

Would I had been, fair Ines,
That gallant cavalier,
Who rode so gaily by thy side,
And whisper'd thee so near! –

Were there no bonny dames at home
Or no true lovers here,
That he should cross the seas to win
The dearest of the dear?

I saw thee, lovely Ines,
Descend along the shore,
With bands of noble gentlemen,
And banners wav'd before;
And gentle youth and maidens gay,
And snowy plumes they wore; –
It would have been a beauteous dream,
– If it had been no more!

Alas, alas, fair Ines,
She went away with song,
With Music waiting on her steps,
And shoutings of the throng;
But some were sad, and felt no mirth,
But only Music's wrong,
In sounds that sang Farewell, Farewell,
To her you've loved so long.

Farewell, farewell, fair Ines,
That vessel never bore
So fair a lady on its deck,
Nor danc'd so light before, –
Alas for pleasure on the sea,
And sorrow on the shore!
The smile that blest one lover's heart
Has broken many more!

The London Magazine, 1823

Ode: Autumn

I saw old Autumn in the misty morn
Stand shadowless like Silence, listening
To silence, for no lonely bird would sing
Into his hollow ear from woods forlorn,
Nor lowly hedge nor solitary thorn; –
Shaking his languid locks all dewy bright
With tangled gossamer that fell by night,
    Pearling his coronet of golden corn.

Where are the songs of Summer? – With the sun,
Oping the dusky eyelids of the south,
Till shade and silence waken up as one,
And Morning sings with a warm odorous mouth.

Where are the merry birds? – Away, away,
On panting wings through the inclement skies,
    Lest owls should prey
    Undazzled at noon-day,
And tear with horny beak their lustrous eyes.

Where are the blooms of Summer? – In the west,
Blushing their last to the last sunny hours,
When the mild Eve by sudden Night is prest
Like tearful Proserpine, snatch'd from her flow'rs
    To a most gloomy breast.
Where is the pride of Summer, – the green prime, –
The many, many leaves all twinkling? – Three
On the moss'd elm; three on the naked lime
Trembling, – and one upon the old oak tree!
    Where is the Dryads' immortality? –
Gone into mournful cypress and dark yew,
Or wearing the long gloomy Winter through
    In the smooth holly's green eternity.

The squirrel gloats o'er his accomplished hoard,
The ants have brimm'd their garners with ripe grain,
  And honey bees have stor'd
The sweets of Summer in their luscious cells;
The swallows all have wing'd across the main;
But here the Autumn melancholy dwells,
  And sighs her tearful spells
Amongst the sunless shadows of the plain.
  Alone, alone,
  Upon a mossy stone,
She sits and reckons up the dead and gone
With the last leaves for a love-rosary,
Whilst all the wither'd world looks drearily,
Like a dim picture of the drowned past
In the hush'd mind's mysterious far away,
Doubtful what ghostly thing will steal the last
Into that distance, grey upon the grey.

O go and sit with her, and be o'ershaded
Under the languid downfall of her hair:
She wears a coronal of flowers faded
Upon her forehead, and a face of care; –
There is enough of wither'd everywhere
To make her bower, – and enough of gloom;
There is enough of sadness to invite,
If only for the rose that died, whose doom
Is Beauty's, – she that with the living bloom
Of conscious cheeks most beautifies the light:
There is enough of sorrowing, and quite
Enough of bitter fruits the earth doth bear, –
Enough of chilly droppings from her bowl;
Enough of fear and shadowy despair,
To frame her cloudy prison for the soul!

The London Magazine, 1823

Sonnet: Silence

There is a silence where hath been no sound,
  There is a silence where no sound may be,
  In the cold grave – under the deep deep sea,
Or in wide desert where no life is found,
Which hath been mute, and still must sleep profound;
  No voice is hush'd – no life treads silently,
  But clouds and cloudy shadows wander free,
That never spoke, over the idle ground:
But in green ruins, in the desolate walls
  Of antique palaces, where Man hath been,
Though the dun fox, or wild hyena, calls,
  And owls, that flit continually between,
Shriek to the echo, and the low winds moan,
There the true Silence is, self-conscious and alone.

The London Magazine, 1823

Sonnet: Written in Keats's 'Endymion'

  I saw pale Dian, sitting by the brink
  Of silver falls, the overflow of fountains
From cloudy steeps; and I grew sad to think
  Endymion's foot was silent on those mountains,
And he but a hush'd name, that Silence keeps
  In dear remembrance, – lonely, and forlorn,
Singing it to herself until she weeps
  Tears that perchance still glisten in the morn; –
And as I mused, in dull imaginings,
  There came a flash of garments, and I knew
The awful Muse by her harmonious wings
  Charming the air to music as she flew –
Anon there rose an echo through the vale
Gave back Endymion in a dream-like tale.

The London Magazine, 1823

Sonnet

It is not death, that sometime in a sigh
This eloquent breath shall take its speechless flight;
That sometime these bright stars, that now reply
In sunlight to the sun, shall set in night;
That this warm conscious flesh shall perish quite,
And all life's ruddy springs forget to flow;
That thoughts shall cease, and the immortal spright
Be lapp'd in alien clay and laid below;
It is not death to know this, – but to know
That pious thoughts, which visit at new graves
In tender pilgrimage, will cease to go
So duly and so oft, – and when grass waves
Over the past-away, there may be then
No resurrection in the minds of men.

The London Magazine, 1823

To a Cold Beauty

Lady, wouldst thou heiress be
    To Winter's cold and cruel part?
When he sets the rivers free,
    Thou dost still lock up thy heart; –
Thou that shouldst outlast the snow,
But in the whiteness of thy brow.

Scorn and cold neglect are made
    For winter gloom and winter wind,
But thou wilt wrong the summer air,
    Breathing it to words unkind, –
Breath which only should belong
To love, to sunlight, and to song!

41

When the little buds unclose,
   Red, and white, and pied, and blue,
And that virgin flow'r, the rose,
   Opes her heart to hold the dew,
Wilt thou lock thy bosom up
With no jewel in its cup?

Let not cold December sit
   Thus in Love's peculiar throne; –
Brooklets are not prison'd now,
   But crystal frosts are all agone,
And that which hangs upon the spray,
It is no snow, but flow'r of May!

The London Magazine, 1823

The Forsaken

The dead are in their silent graves,
And the dew is cold above,
And the living weep and sigh,
Over dust that once was love.

Once I only wept the dead,
But now the living cause my pain:
How couldst thou steal me from my tears,
To leave me to my tears again?

My Mother rests beneath the sod, –
Her rest is calm and very deep:
I wish'd that she could see our loves, –
But now I gladden in her sleep.

Last night unbound my raven locks,
The morning saw them turn'd to gray,
Once they were black and well-belov'd,
But thou art chang'd, – and so are they!

The useless lock I gave thee once,
To gaze upon and think of me,
Was ta'en with smiles, – but this was torn
In sorrow that I send to thee!

1824

Song

O Lady, leave thy silken thread
And flowery tapestrie,
There's living roses on the bush,
And blossoms on the tree;
Stoop where thou wilt, thy careless hand
Some random bud will meet;
Thou canst not tread but thou wilt find
The daisy at thy feet.

'Tis like the birthday of the world,
When earth was born in bloom;
The light is made of many dyes,
The air is all perfume;
There's crimson buds, and white and blue –
The very rainbow show'rs
Have turn'd to blossoms where they fell,
And sown the earth with flow'rs.

There's fairy tulips in the East,
The garden of the sun;
The very streams reflect the hues,
And blossom as they run:
While morn opes like a crimson rose,
Still wet with pearly showers;
Then, lady, leave thy silken thread
Thou twinest into flow'rs!

Forget-me-Not, 1824

The Two Swans
lines 59-80

The distant shores show dimly and remote,
Made of a deeper mist, – serene and grey, –
And slow and mute the cloudy shadows float
Over the gloomy wave, and pass away,
Chased by the silver beams that on their margins play.

And bright and silvery the willows sleep
Over the shady verge – no mad winds tease
Their hoary heads; but quietly they weep
Their sprinkling leaves – half fountains and half trees:
There lilies be – and fairer than all these,
A solitary Swan her breast of snow
Launches against the wave that seems to freeze
Into a chaste reflection, still below,
Twin shadow of herself wherever she may go.

And forth she paddles in the very noon
Of solemn midnight, like an elfin thing
Charm'd into being by the argent moon –
Whose silver light for love of her fair wing

Goes with her in the shade, still worshipping
Her dainty plumage: – all around her grew
A radiant circlet, like a fairy ring;
And all behind, a tiny little clue
Of light to guide her back across the waters blue.

And sure she is no meaner than a fay,
Redeem'd from sleepy death, for beauty's sake,
By old ordainment: – silent as she lay,
Touch'd by a moonlight wand I saw her wake,
And cut her leafy slough and so forsake
The verdant prison of her lily peers,
That slept amidst the stars upon the lake –
A breathing shape – restored to human fears,
And new-born love and grief – self-conscious of her tears.

New Monthly Magazine, 1824

In 1825 Hood, in collaboration with J.H. Reynolds, published anonymously, a series of topical *Odes and Addresses to Great People*. They
were prefaced by a quotation from Goldsmith's *Citizen of the World*: 'Catching
all the oddities, the whimsies, the absurdities, and the littlenesses of
conscious greatness by the way.'

Ode to Mr Graham, the aeronaut.
lines 1-78

Dear Graham, whilst the busy crowd,
The vain, the wealthy, and the proud,
    Their meaner flights pursue,
Let us cast off the foolish ties
That bind us to the earth, and rise
    And take a bird's-eye view! –

A few more whiffs of my segar
And then, in Fancy's airy car,
     Have with thee for the skies: –
How oft this fragrant smoke upcurl'd
Hath borne me from this little world,
     And all that in it lies! –

Away! – away! – the bubble fills –
Farewell to earth and all its hills! –
     We seem to cut the wind! –
So high we mount, so swift we go,
The chimney tops are far below,
     The Eagle's left behind! –

Ah me! my brain begins to swim! –
The world is growing rather dim;
     The steeples and the trees –
My wife is getting very small!
I cannot see my babe at all! –
     The Dolland, if you please!

Do, Graham, let me have a quiz,
Lord! what a Lilliput it is,
     That little world of Mogg's!
Are those the London Docks? – that channel,
The mighty Thames? – a proper kennel
     For that small Isle of Dogs! –

What is that seeming tea-urn there?
That fairy dome, St Paul's! – I swear,
     Wren must have been a Wren! –
And that small stripe? – it cannot be
The City Road! – Good lack! to see
     The little ways of men!

Little, indeed! – my eyeballs ache
To find a turnpike. – I must take
    Their tolls upon my trust! –
And where is mortal labour gone?
Look, Graham, for a little stone
    Mac Adamized to dust!

Look at the horses! – less than flies! –
Oh, what a waste it was of sighs
    To wish to be a Mayor!
What is the honour? – none at all,
    One's honour must be very small
    For such a civic chair! –

And there's Guildhall! – 'tis far aloof –
Methinks I fancy thro' the roof
    Its little guardian Gogs,
Like penny dolls – a tiny show! –
Well, I must say they're ruled below
    By very little logs! –

Oh! Graham, how the upper air
Alters the standards of compare;
    One of our silken flags
Would cover London all about –
Nay then – let's even empty out
    Another brace of bags!

Now for a glass of bright champagne
Above the clouds! – Come let us drain
    A bumper as we go! –
But hold! – for God's sake do not cant
The cork away – unless you want
    To brain your friends below.

Think! what a mob of little men
Are crawling just within our ken,
    Like mites upon a cheese! –
Pshaw! – how the foolish sight rebukes
Ambitious thoughts! – can there be *Dukes*
    Of *Gloster* such as these! –

Oh! what is glory? – what is fame?
Hark to the little mob's acclaim,
    'Tis nothing but a hum! –
A few near gnats would trump as loud
As all the shouting of a crowd
    That has so far to come! –

A **Friendly** *Address to Mrs. Fry* In *Newgate*
lines 81-120

Ah, who can tell how hard it is to teach
    Miss Nancy Dawson on her bed of straw –
To make long Sal sew up the endless breach
    She made in manners – to write heaven's own law
On hearts of granite. – Nay, how hard to preach,
    In cells, that are not memory's – to draw
The moral thread, thro' the immoral eye
Of blunt Whitechapel natures, Mrs. Fry!

In vain you teach them baby-work within:
    'Tis but a clumsy botchery of crime;
'Tis but a tedious darning of old sin –
    Come out yourself, and stitch up souls in time –
It is too late for scouring to begin
    When virtue's ravell'd out, when all the prime
Is worn away, and nothing sound remains;
You'll fret the fabric out before the stains!

48

I like your chocolate, good Mistress Fry!
    I like your cookery in every way;
I like your shrove-tide service and supply;
    I like to hear your sweet *Pandeans* play;
I like the pity in your full-brimm'd eye;
    I like your carriage and your silken grey,
Your dove-like habits, and your silent preaching;
    But I don't like your Newgatory teaching.

Come out of Newgate, Mrs. Fry! Repair
    Abroad, and find your pupils in the streets.
O, come abroad into the wholesome air,
    And take your moral place, before Sin seats
Her wicked self in the Professor's chair.
    Suppose some morals raw! the true receipt's
To dress them in the pan, but do not try
To cook them in the fire, good Mrs. Fry!

Put on your decent bonnet, and come out!
    Good lack! the ancients did not set up schools
In jail – but at the *Porch*! hinting, no doubt,
    That Vice should have a lesson in the rules
Before 'twas whipt by law. – O come about,
    Good Mrs. Fry! and set up forms and stools
All down the Old Bailey, and thro' Newgate-street,
But not in Mr. Wontner's proper seat!...

lines 145-152

...In brief, – Oh teach the child its moral rote,
    Not *in* the way from which it won't depart, –
But *out* – out – out! Oh, bid it walk remote!
    And if the skies are clos'd against the smart,

49

Ev'n let him wear the single-breasted coat,
     For that ensureth singleness of heart. –
Do what you will, his every want supply,
Keep him – but *out* of Newgate, Mrs. Fry!

Ode to Joseph Grimaldi, Senior

'This fellow's wise enough to play the fool,
And to do that well craves a kind of wit.'
                              Twelfth Night.

Joseph! they say thou'st left the stage,
     To toddle down the hill of life,
And taste the flannell'd ease of age,
     Apart from pantomimic strife –
'Retir'd – (for Young would call it so) –
The world shut out' – in Pleasant Row!

And hast thou really wash'd at last
     From each white cheek the red half moon?
And all thy public Clownship cast,
     To play the private Pantaloon?
All youth – all ages – yet to be,
Shall have a heavy miss of thee!

Thou didst not preach to make us wise –
     Thou hadst no finger in our schooling –
Thou didst not 'lure us to the skies' –
     Thy simple, simple trade was – Fooling!
And yet, Heav'n knows! we could – we can
Much 'better spare a better man!'

Oh, had it pleas'd the gout to take
    The reverend Croly from the stage,
Or Southey, for our quiet's sake,
    Or Mr. Fletcher, Cupid's sage,
Or, damme! namby pamby Poole, –
Or any other clown or fool!

Go, Dibdin – all that bear the name,
    Go Byeway Highway man! go! go!
Go Skeffy – man of painted fame,
    But leave thy partner, painted Joe!
I could bear Kirby on the wane,
Or Signor Paulo with a sprain!

Had Joseph Wilfred Parkins made
    His grey hairs scarce in private peace –
Had Waithman sought a rural shade –
    Or Cobbett ta'en a turnpike lease –
Or Lisle Bowles gone to *Balaam* Hill –
I think I could be cheerful still!

Had Medwin left off, to his praise,
    Dead lion kicking, like – a friend!
Had long, long Irving gone his ways,
    To muse on death at *Ponder's End* –
Or Lady Morgan taken leave
Of Letters – still I might not grieve!

But, Joseph – everybody's Jo! –
    Is gone – and grieve I will and must!
As Hamlet did for Yorick, so
    Will I for thee, (tho' not yet dust,)
And talk as he did when he miss'd
The kissing-crust that he had kiss'd!

Ah, where is now thy rolling head!
   Thy winking, reeling, *drunken* eyes,
(As old Catullus would have said,)
   Thy oven-mouth, that swallow'd pies –
Enormous hunger – monstrous drowth!
Thy pockets greedy as thy mouth!

Ah, where thy ears, so often cuff'd! –
   Thy funny, flapping, filching hands! –
Thy partridge body, always stuff'd
   With waifs, and strays, and contrabands! –
Thy foot – like Berkeley's *Foote* – for why?
'Twas often made to wipe an eye!

Ah, where thy legs – that witty pair!
   For 'great wits jump' – and so did they!
Lord! how they leap'd in lamp-light air!
   Caper'd – and bounc'd – and strode away! –
That years should tame the legs – alack!
I've seen spring through an Almanack!

But bounds will have their bound – the shocks
   Of Time will cramp the nimblest toes;
And those that frisk'd in silken clocks
   May look to limp in fleecy hose –
One only – (Champion of the ring)
Could ever make his Winter, – Spring!

And gout, that holds no odds between
   The toe of Czar and toe of Clown,
Will visit – but I did not mean
   To moralize, though I am grown
Thus sad, – Thy going seem'd to beat
A muffled drum for Fun's retreat!

And, may be – 'tis no time to smother
   A sigh, when two prime wags of London,
Are gone – thou, Joseph, one – the other,
   A Joe! – 'sic transit gloria *Munden*!'
A third departure some insist on, –
Stage-apoplexy threatens Liston! –

Nay, then, let Sleeping Beauty sleep
   With ancient *'Dozey'* to the dregs –
Let Mother Goose wear mourning deep,
   And put a hatchment o'er her eggs!
Let Farley weep – for Magic's man
Is gone, – his Christmas Caliban!

Let Kemble, Forbes, and Willet rain,
   As tho' they walk'd behind thy bier, –
For since thou wilt not play again,
   What matters, – if in heav'n or here!
   Or in thy grave, or in thy bed!
There's *Quick*, might just as well be dead!

Oh, how will thy departure cloud
   The lamp-light of the little breast!
The Christmas child will grieve aloud
   To miss his broadest friend and best, –
Poor urchin! what avails to him
The cold New Monthly's *Ghost of Grimm*?

For who like thee could ever stride
   Some dozen paces to the mile! –
The motley, medley coach provide –
   Or like Joe Frankenstein compile
The *vegetable man* complete! –
A proper *Covent Garden* feat!

Oh, who like thee could ever drink,
　　Or eat – swill, swallow – bolt – and choke!
Nod, weep, and hiccup – sneeze and wink? –
Thy very yawn was quite a joke!
Tho' Joseph, Junior, acts not ill,
　　'There's no Fool like the old Fool' still!

Joseph, farewell! dear funny Joe!
　　We met with mirth, we part in pain!
For many a long, long year must go,
　　Ere Fun can see thy like again –
For Nature does not keep great stores
Of perfect Clowns – that are not *Boors*!

An Address to the Steam Washing Company
lines 53-91

Lo, then, the poor laundress, all wretched she stands,
Instead of a counterpane wringing her hands!
All haggard and pinch'd, going down in life's vale,
With no faggot for burning, like Allan-a-dale!
No smoke from her flue – and no steam from her pane,
Where once she watch'd heaven, fearing God and the rain –
Or gaz'd o'er her bleach-field so fairly engross'd,
Till the lines wander'd idle from pillar to post!
Ah, where are the playful young pinners – ah, where
The harlequin quilts that cut capers in air –
The brisk waltzing stockings – the white and the black,
That danc'd on the tight-rope, or swung on the slack –
The light sylph-like garments so tenderly pinn'd,
That blew into shape and embodied the wind!
There was white on the grass – there was white on the spray –
Her garden it look'd like a garden of May!

But now all is dark – not a shirt's on a shrub –
You've ruin'd her prospects in life, Mr Scrub!
You've ruin'd her custom – now families drop her –
From her silver reduc'd – nay reduc'd her from *copper*!
The last of her washing is done at her eye,
One poor little kerchief that never gets dry!
From mere lack of linen she can't lay a cloth,
And boils neither barley nor alkaline broth –
But her children come round her as victuals grow scant,
And recall, with foul faces, the source of their want –
When she thinks of their poor little mouths to be fed,
And then thinks of her trade that is utterly dead,
And even its pearlashes laid in the grave –
Whilst her tub is a dry rotting, stave after stave,
And the greatest of Coopers, ev'n he that they dub
Sir Astley, can't bind up her heart or her tub, –
Need you wonder, when steam has depriv'd her of bread,
If she prays that the evil may visit *your* head –
Nay, scald all the heads of your Washing Committee, –
If she wishes you all the soot blacks of the city –
In short, not to mention all plagues without number,
If she wishes you all in the *Wash* at the Humber!

Odes and Addresses, 1825

The Water Lady

Alas, the moon should ever beam
To show what man should never see! –
I saw a maiden on a stream,
And fair was she!

I staid awhile, to see her throw
Her tresses back, that all beset
The fair horizon of her brow
With clouds of jet.

I staid a little while to view
Her cheek, that wore in place of red
The bloom of water, tender blue,
Daintily spread.

I staid to watch, a little space,
Her parted lips if she would sing;
The waters closed above her face
With many a ring.

And still I staid a little more,
Alas! she never comes again;
I throw my flow'rs from the shore,
And watch in vain.

I know my life will fade away,
I know that I must vainly pine,
For I am made of mortal clay,
But she's divine!

Forget-me-Not, 1826

The Last Man

'Twas in the year two thousand and one,
A pleasant morning of May,
I sat on the gallows-tree all alone,
A chaunting a merry lay, –
To think how the pest had spared my life,
To sing with the larks that day!

When up the heath came a jolly knave,
Like a scarecrow, all in rags:
It made me crow to see his old duds
All abroad in the wind like flags: –
So up he came to the timbers' foot
And pitch'd down his greasy bags. –

Good Lord! how blythe the old beggar was!
At pulling out his scraps, –
The very sight of his broken orts
Made a work in his wrinkled chaps:
'Come down,' says he, 'you Newgate bird,
And have a taste of my snaps!'

Then down the rope, like a tar from the mast,
I slided and by him stood;
But I wished myself on the gallows again
When I smelt that beggar's food,
A foul beef-bone, and a mouldy crust;
'Oh!' quoth he, 'the heavens are good!'

Then after this grace he cast him down:
Says I, 'You'll get sweeter air
A pace or two off, on the windward side,'
For the felons' bones lay there.
But he only laugh'd at the empty skulls,
And offered them part of his fare.

'I never harm'd *them*, and they won't harm me:
Let the proud and the rich be cravens!'
I did not like that strange beggar man,
He look'd so up at the heavens.
Anon he shook out his empty old poke;
'There's the crumbs', saith he, 'for the ravens!'

It made me angry to see his face,
It had such a jesting look;
But while I made up my mind to speak,
A small case-bottle he took:
Quoth he, 'though I gather the green water-cress,
My drink is not of the brook!'

Full manners-like he tender'd the dram;
Oh, it came of a dainty cask!
But, whenever it came to his turn to pull,
'Your leave, good sir, I must ask;
But I always wipe the brim with my sleeve,
When a hangman sups at my flask!'

And then he laugh'd so loudly and long,
The churl was quite out of breath;
I thought the very Old One was come
To mock me before my death,
And wish'd I had buried the dead-men's bones
That were lying about the heath!

But the beggar gave me a jolly clap –
'Come let us pledge each other,
For all the wide world is dead beside,
And we are brother and brother –
I've a yearning for thee in my heart,
As if we had come of one mother.

'I've a yearning for thee in my heart
That almost makes me weep,
For as I pass'd from town to town
The folks were all stone-asleep, –
But when I saw thee sitting aloft,
It made me both laugh and leap!'

Now a curse (I thought) be on his love,
And a curse upon his mirth, –
An' if it were not for that beggar man
I'd be the King of the earth, –
But I promis'd myself an hour should come
To make him rue his birth –

So down we sat and bous'd again
Till the sun was in mid-sky,
When, just when the gentle west-wind came,
We hearken'd a dismal cry;
'Up, up, on the tree,' quoth the beggar man,
'Till these horrible dogs go by!'

And, lo! from the forest's far-off skirts,
They came all yelling for gore,
A hundred hounds pursuing at once,
And a panting hart before,
Till he sunk down at the gallows' foot,
And there his haunches they tore!

His haunches they tore, without a horn
To tell when the chase was done;
And there was not a single scarlet coat
To flaunt it in the sun! –
I turn'd, and look'd at the beggar man,
And his tears dropt one by one!

And with curses sore he chid at the hounds,
Till the last dropt out of sight,
'Anon', saith he, 'Let's down again,
And ramble for our delight,
For the world's all free, and we may choose
A right cozie barn for to-night!'

With that, he set up his staff on end,
And it fell with the point due West;
So we far'd that way to a city great,
Where the folks had died of the pest –
It was fine to enter in house and hall
Wherever it liked me best;

For the porters all were stiff and cold,
And could not lift their heads;
And when we came where their masters lay,
The rats leapt out of the beds;
The grandest palaces in the land
Were as free as workhouse sheds.

But the beggar man made a mumping face,
And knocked at every gate:
It made me curse to hear how he whined,
So our fellowship turned to hate,
And I bade him walk the world by himself,
For I scorn'd so humble a mate!

So *he* turn'd right, and *I* turn'd left,
As if we had never met;
And I chose a fair stone house for myself,
For the city was all to let;
And for three brave holidays drank my fill
Of the choicest that I could get.

And because my jerkin was coarse and worn,
I got me a properer vest;
It was purple velvet, stitch'd o'er with gold,
And a shining star at the breast! –
'Twas enough to fetch old Joan from her grave
To see me so purely drest!

But Joan was dead and under the mould,
And every buxom lass;
In vain I watch'd, at the window pane
For a Christian soul to pass!
But sheep and kine wander'd up the street,
And browz'd on the new-come grass. –

When lo! I spied the old beggar man,
And lustily he did sing! –
His rags were lapp'd in a scarlet cloak,
And a crown he had like a King;
So he stept right up before my gate
And danc'd me a saucy fling!

Heaven mend us all! – but, within my mind,
I had killed him then and there;
To see him lording so braggart-like
That was born to his beggar's fare,
And how he had stolen the royal crown
His betters were meant to wear.

But God forbid that a thief should die
Without his share of the laws!
So I nimbly whipt my tackle out,
And soon tied up his claws, –
I was judge myself, and jury, and all,
And solemnly tried the cause.

But the beggar man would not plead, but cried
Like a babe without its corals,
For he knew how hard it is apt to go
When the law and a thief have quarrels, –
There was not a Christian soul alive
To speak a word for his morals.

Oh, how gaily I doff'd my costly gear,
And put on my work-day clothes;
I was tired of such a long Sunday life, –
And never was one of the sloths;
But the beggar man grumbled a weary deal,
And made many crooked mouths.

So I haul'd him off to the gallows' foot,
And blinded him in his bags;
'Twas a weary job to heave him up;
For a doom'd man always lags;
But by ten of the clock he was off his legs
In the wind, and airing his rags!

So there he hung, and there I stood,
The LAST MAN left alive,
To have my own will of all the earth:
Quoth I, now I shall thrive!
But when was ever honey made
With one bee in a hive?

My conscience began to gnaw my heart,
Before the day was done,
For other men's lives had all gone out,
Like candles in the sun! –
But it seem'd as if I had broke, at last,
A thousand necks in one!

So I went and cut his body down
To bury it decentlie; –
God send there were any good soul alive
To do the like by me!
But the wild dogs came with terrible speed,
And bade me up the tree!

My sight was like a drunkard's sight,
And my head began to swim,
To see their jaws all white with foam,
Like the ravenous ocean brim; –
But when the wild dogs trotted away
Their jaws were bloody and grim!

Their jaws were bloody and grim, good Lord!
But the beggar man where was he? –
There was naught of him but some ribbons of rags
Below the gallows' tree! –
I know the Devil, when I am dead,
Will send his hounds for me! –

I've buried my babies one by one,
And dug the deep hole for Joan,
And covered the faces of kith and kin,
And felt the old churchyard stone
Go cold to my heart, full many a time,
But I never felt so lone!

For the lion and Adam were company,
And the tiger him beguiled:
But the simple kine are foes to my life,
And the household brutes are wild.
If the veriest cur would lick my hand,
I could love it like a child!

And the beggar man's ghost besets my dream,
At night to make me madder, –
And my wretched conscience within my breast,
Is like a stinging adder; –
I sigh when I pass the gallows' foot,
And look at the rope and ladder! –

For hanging looks sweet, – but, alas! in vain
My desperate fancy begs, –
I must turn my cup of sorrows quite up,
And drink it to the dregs, –
For there is not another man alive,
In the world to pull my legs!

Whims and Oddities, 1826

I remember, I remember

I remember, I remember,
The house where I was born,
The little window where the sun
Came peeping in at morn;
He never came a wink too soon,
Nor brought too long a day,
But now, I often wish the night
Had borne my breath away!

I remember, I remember,
The roses, red and white,
The vi'lets, and the lily-cups,
Those flowers made of light!
The lilacs where the robin built,
And where my brother set
The laburnum on his birthday, –
The tree is living yet!

I remember, I remember,
Where I was used to swing,
And thought the air must rush as fresh
To swallows on the wing;

My spirit flew in feathers then,
That is so heavy now,
And summer pools could hardly cool
The fever on my brow!

I remember, I remember,
The fir trees dark and high;
I used to think their slender tops
Were close against the sky:
It was a childish ignorance,
But now 'tis little joy
To know I'm farther off from heav'n
Than when I was a boy.

Friendship's Offering, 1826

[*In Memoriam*]

Little eyes that scarce did see,
  Little lips that never smiled;
  Alas! my little dear dead child,
Death is thy father, and not me,
I but embraced thee, soon as he.

May, 1827
[unpublished]

Bianca's Dream

A Venetian Story

lines 177-end

The fair Bianca has for a long time remained impervious to her suitors, among them the devoted Julio. One night she dreams of looking in her mirror and seeing the gradual changes Time will execute on her beauty:

So Time with fair Bianca dealt, and made
    Her shape a bow, that once was like an arrow;
His iron hand upon her spine he laid,
    And twisted all awry her 'winsome marrow'.
In truth it was a change! – she had obey'd
    The holy Pope before her chest grew narrow,
But spectacles and palsy seem'd to make her
Something between a Glassite and a Quaker.

Her grief and gall meanwhile were quite extreme,
    And she had ample reason for her trouble;
For what sad maiden can endure to seem
    Set in for singleness, tho' growing double?
The fancy madden'd her; but now the dream,
    Grown thin by getting bigger, like a bubble,
Burst, – but still left some fragments of its size,
That, like the soapsuds, smarted in her eyes.

And here – just here – as she began to heed
    The real world, her clock chimed out its score;
A clock it was of the Venetian breed,
    That cried the hour from one to twenty-four;
The works moreover standing in some need
    Of workmanship, it struck some dozen more;
A warning voice that clench'd Bianca's fears,
Such strokes referring doubtless to her years.

At fifteen years she was but half a nun,
    By twenty she had quite renounced the veil;
She thought of Julio just at twenty-one,
    And thirty made her very sad and pale,
To paint that ruin where her charms would run;
    At forty all the maid began to fail,
And thought no higher, as the late dream cross'd her,
Of single blessedness, than single Gloster.

And so Bianca changed; – the next sweet even,
    With Julio in a black Venetian bark,
Row'd slow and stealthily – the hour, eleven,
    Just sounding from the tow'r of old St. Mark,
She sate with eyes turn'd quietly to heav'n,
    Perchance rejoicing in the grateful dark
That veil'd her blushing cheek – for Julio brought her,
Of course, to break the ice upon the water.

But what a puzzle is one's serious mind
    To open; – oysters, when the ice is thick,
Are not so difficult and disinclin'd;
    And Julio felt the declaration stick
About his throat in a most awful kind;
    However, he contrived by bits to pick
His trouble forth, – much like a rotten cork
Grop'd from a long-neck'd bottle with a fork.

But love is still the quickest of all readers;
    And Julio spent besides those signs profuse
That English telegraphs and foreign pleaders,
    In help of language, are so apt to use;
Arms, shoulders, fingers, all were interceders,
    Nods, shrugs, and bends, – Bianca could not choose
But soften to his suit with more facility,
He told his story with so much agility.

'Be thou my park and I will be thy dear,
  (So he began at last to speak or quote;)
Be thou my bark and I thy gondolier,
  (For passion takes this figurative note;)
Be thou my light, and I thy chandelier;
  Be thou my dove, and I will be thy cote:
My lily be, and I will be thy river;
Be thou my life – and I will be thy liver.'

This, with more tender logic of the kind,
  He pour'd into her small and shell-like ear,
That timidly against his lips inclin'd;
  Meanwhile her eyes glanced on the silver sphere
That even now began to steal behind
  A dewy vapour, which was lingering near,
Wherein the dull moon crept all dim and pale,
Just like a virgin putting on the veil: –

Bidding adieu to all her sparks – the stars,
  That erst had woo'd and worshipp'd in her train,
Saturn and Hesperus, and gallant Mars –
  Never to flirt with heavenly eyes again.
Meanwhile, remindful of the convent bars,
  Bianca did not watch these signs in vain,
But turn'd to Julio at the dark eclipse,
With words, like verbal kisses, on her lips.

He took the hint full speedily, and, back'd
  By love, and night, and the occasion's meetness,
Bestow'd a something on her cheek that smack'd
  (Tho' quite in silence) of ambrosial sweetness;
That made her think all other kisses lack'd
  Till then, but what she knew not, of completeness:
Being used but sisterly salutes to feel,
Insipid things – like sandwiches of veal.

He took her hand, and soon she felt him wring
   The pretty fingers all instead of one;
Anon his stealthy arm began to cling
   About her waist that had been clasp'd by none;
Their dear confessions I forbear to sing,
   Since cold description would but be outrun;
For bliss and Irish watches have the pow'r,
In twenty minutes, to lose half an hour!

Whims and Oddities, 1827

Ballad

It was not in the winter
   Our loving lot was cast!
It was the time of roses,
   We plucked them as we passed!

That churlish season never frowned
   On early lovers yet! –
Oh no – the world was newly crowned
   With flowers, when first we met.

'Twas twilight, and I bade you go,
   But still you held me fast; –
It was the time of roses, –
   We plucked them as we passed!

What else could peer my glowing cheek
   That tears began to stud? –
And when I asked the like of Love
   You snatched a damask bud, –

And oped it to the dainty core
　　Still glowing to the last: –
It was the time of roses,
　　We plucked them as we passed!
Literary Souvenir, 1827

Ruth

She stood breast high amid the corn,
Clasp'd by the golden light of morn,
Like the sweetheart of the sun,
Who many a glowing kiss had won.

On her cheek an autumn flush,
Deeply ripened; – such a blush
In the midst of brown was born,
Like red poppies grown with corn.

Round her eyes her tresses fell,
Which were blackest none could tell,
But long lashes veil'd a light,
That had else been all too bright.

And her hat, with shady brim,
Made her tressy forehead dim; –
Thus she stood amid the stooks,
Praising God with sweetest looks: –

Sure, I said, heav'n did not mean,
Where I reap thou shouldst but glean,
Lay thy sheaf adown and come,
Share my harvest and my home.
Forget-me-Not, 1827

On Mistress Nicely, a Pattern for Housekeepers

*Written after seeing Mrs Davenport in
the character, at Covent Garden.*

She was a woman peerless in her station,
   With household virtues wedded to her name;
   Spotless in linen, grass-bleach'd in her fame,
And pure and clear-starch'd in her conversation;
Thence in my Castle of Imagination
   She dwells for evermore, the dainty dame,
   To keep all airy draperies from shame,
And all dream furnitures in preservation:
   There walketh she with keys quite silver bright,
In perfect hose, and shoes of seemly black,
   Apron and stomacher of lily-white,
And decent order follows in her track:
   The burnish'd plate grows lustrous in her sight,
And polish'd floors and tables shine her back.

Literary Magnet, 1827

Sonnet

Love, dearest Lady, such as I would speak,
Lives not within the humour of the eye; –
Not being but an outward phantasy,
That skims the surface of a tinted cheek, –
Else it would wane with beauty, and grow weak,
As if the rose made summer, – and so lie
Among the perishable things that die,
Unlike the love which I would give and seek:
Whose health is of no hue – to feel decay
With cheeks' decay, that have a rosy prime.

Love is its own great loveliness alway,
And takes new lustre from the touch of time;
Its bough owns no December and no May,
But bears its blossom into Winter's clime.

The Plea of the Midsummer Fairies, 1827

Song
for Music

A lake and a fairy boat
To sail in the moonlight clear, –
And merrily we would float
From the dragons that watch us here!

Thy gown should be snow-white silk,
And strings of orient pearls,
Like gossamers dipp'd in milk,
Should twine with thy raven curls!

Red rubies should deck thy hands,
And diamonds should be thy dow'r –
But Fairies have broke their wands,
And wishing has lost its pow'r!

The Plea of the Midsummer Fairies, 1827

On the Death of the Giraffe

They say, God wot!
She died upon the spot;
But then in spots she was so rich, –
I wonder which?

Forget-me-Not, 1828

The Dream of Eugene Aram, the Murderer

'Twas in the prime of summer time,
  An evening calm and cool,
And four and twenty happy boys
  Came bounding out of school:
There were some that ran and some that leapt,
  Like troutlets in a pool.

Away they sped with gamesome minds,
  And souls untouched by sin;
To a level mead they came, and there
  They drave the wickets in:
Pleasantly shone the setting sun
  Over the town of Lynn.

Like sportive deer they cours'd about,
  And shouted as they ran, –
Turning to mirth all things of earth,
  As only boyhood can;
But the Usher sat remote from all,
  A melancholy man!

His hat was off, his vest apart,
  To catch heaven's blessed breeze;
For a burning thought was in his brow,
  And his bosom ill at ease:
So he lean'd his head on his hands, and read
  The book between his knees!

Leaf after leaf, he turn'd it o'er,
  Nor ever glanc'd aside,
For the peace of his soul he read that book
  In the golden eventide:
Much study had made him very lean,
  And pale, and leaden-ey'd.

At last he shut the ponderous tome,
  With a fast and fervent grasp
He strained the dusky covers close,
  And fixed the brazen hasp:
'Oh, God! could I so close my mind,
  And clasp it with a clasp!'

Then leaping on his feet upright,
  Some moody turns he took, –
Now up the mead, then down the mead,
  And past a shady nook, –
And, lo! he saw a little boy
  That pored upon a book!

'My gentle lad, what is't you read –
  Romance or fairy fable?
Or is it some historic page,
  Of kings and crowns unstable?'
The young boy gave an upward glance, –
  'It is "The Death of Abel".'

The Usher took six hasty strides,
  As smit with sudden pain, –
Six hasty strides beyond the place,
  Then slowly back again;
And down he sat beside the lad,
  And talked with him of Cain;

And, long since then, of bloody men,
  Whose deeds tradition saves;
Of lonely folk cut off unseen,
  And hid in sudden graves;
Of horrid stabs, in groves forlorn,
  And murder done in caves;

And how the sprites of injur'd men
   Shriek upward from the sod, –
Aye, how the ghostly hand will point
   To show the burial clod;
And unknown facts of guilty acts
   Are seen in dreams from God!

He told how murderers walk the earth
   Beneath the curse of Cain, –
With crimson clouds before their eyes,
   And flames about their brain:
For blood has left upon their souls
   Its everlasting stain!

'And well,' quoth he, 'I know, for truth,
   Their pangs must be extreme, –
Woe, woe, unutterable woe, –
   Who spill life's sacred stream!
For why? methought, last night, I wrought
   A murder, in a dream!

'One that had never done me wrong –
   A feeble man, and old;
I led him to a lonely field, –
   The moon shone clear and cold:
Now here, said I, this man shall die,
   And I will have his gold!

'Two sudden blows with a ragged stick,
   And one with a heavy stone,
One hurried gash with a hasty knife, –
   And then the deed was done:
There was nothing lying at my foot
   But lifeless flesh and bone!

'Nothing but lifeless flesh and bone,
    That could not do me ill;
And yet I fear'd him all the more,
    For lying there so still:
There was a manhood in his look,
    That murder could not kill!

'And, lo! the universal air
    Seem'd lit with ghastly flame; –
Ten thousand thousand dreadful eyes
    Were looking down in blame:
I took the dead man by his hand,
    And call'd upon his name!

'Oh, God! it made me quake to see
    Such sense within the slain!
But when I touch'd the lifeless clay,
    The blood gush'd out amain!
For every clot, a burning spot,
    Was scorching in my brain!

'My head was like an ardent coal,
    My heart as solid ice;
My wretched, wretched soul, I knew,
    Was at the Devil's price:
A dozen times I groan'd; the dead
    Had never groan'd but twice!

'And now, from forth the frowning sky,
    From the Heaven's topmost height,
I heard a voice – the awful voice
    Of the blood-avenging Sprite: –
"Thou guilty man! take up thy dead,
    And hide it from my sight!"

'I took the dreary body up,
    And cast it in a stream, –
A sluggish water, black as ink,
    The depth was so extreme; –
My gentle Boy, remember this
    Is nothing but a dream!

'Down went the corse with a hollow plunge,
    And vanish'd in the pool;
Anon I cleans'd my bloody hands,
    And wash'd my forehead cool,
And sat among the urchins young
    That evening in the school.

'Oh, Heaven, to think of their white souls,
    And mine so black and grim!
I could not share in childish prayer,
    Nor join in Evening Hymn:
Like a Devil of the Pit, I seem'd,
    'Mid holy Cherubim!

'And Peace went with them, one and all,
    And each calm pillow spread;
But Guilt was my grim Chamberlain
    That lighted me to bed;
And drew my midnight curtains round
    With fingers bloody red!

'All night I lay in agony,
    In anguish dark and deep;
My fever'd eyes I dared not close,
    But stared aghast at Sleep:
For Sin had render'd unto her
    The keys of Hell to keep!

'All night I lay in agony,
  From weary chime to chime,
With one besetting horrid hint,
  That racked me all the time, –
A mighty yearning, like the first
  Fierce impulse unto crime!

'One stern tyrannic thought, that made
  All other thoughts its slave;
Stronger and stronger every pulse
  Did that temptation crave, –
Still urging me to go and see
  The Dead Man in his grave!

'Heavily I rose up, as soon
  As light was in the sky,
And sought the black, accursed pool
  With a wild misgiving eye;
And I saw the Dead in the river bed,
  For the faithless stream was dry!

'Merrily rose the lark, and shook
  The dew-drop from its wing;
But I never mark'd its morning flight,
  I never heard it sing:
For I was stooping once again
  Under the horrid thing.

'With breathless speed, like a soul in chase,
  I took him up and ran; –
There was no time to dig a grave
  Before the day began:
In a lonesome wood, with heaps of leaves,
  I hid the murder'd man!

'And all that day I read in school,
     But my thought was otherwhere;
As soon as the mid-day task was done,
     In secret I was there:
And a mighty wind had swept the leaves,
     And still the corse was bare!

'Then down I cast me on my face,
     And first began to weep,
For I knew my secret then was one
     That earth refused to keep:
Or land, or sea, though he should be
     Ten thousand fathoms deep.

'So wills the fierce avenging Sprite,
     Till blood for blood atones!
Ay, though he's buried in a cave,
     And trodden down with stones,
And years have rotted off his flesh, –
     The world shall see his bones!

'Oh, God! that horrid, horrid dream
     Besets me now awake!
Again – again, with a dizzy brain,
     The human life I take;
And my right hand grows raging hot,
     Like Cranmer's at the stake.

'And still no peace for the restless clay,
     Will wave or mould allow;
The horrid thing pursues my soul, –
     It stands before me now!'
The fearful Boy look'd up, and saw
     Huge drops upon his brow.

That very night, while gentle sleep
   The urchin eyelids kiss'd,
Two stern-faced men set out from Lynn,
   Through the cold and heavy mist;
And Eugene Aram walked between,
   With gyves upon his wrist.

The Gem, 1829

The Death Bed

We watch'd her breathing through the night,
   Her breathing soft and low,
As in her breast the wave of life
   Kept heaving to and fro.

So silently we seem'd to speak,
   So slowly moved about,
As we had lent her half our powers
   To eke her living out.

Our very hopes belied our fears,
   Our fears our hopes belied –
We thought her dying when she slept,
   And sleeping when she died.

For when the morn came dim and sad,
   And chill with early showers,
Her quiet eyelids closed – she had
   Another morn than ours.

Englishman's Magazine, 1831

Sonnet

Time was, I sat upon a lofty stool,
At lofty desk, and with a clerkly pen
Began each morning, at the stroke of ten,
To write in Bell & Co.'s commercial school;
In Warnford Court, a shady nook and cool,
The favourite retreat of mechantmen;
Yet would my pen turn vagrant even then,
And take stray dips in the Castalian pool.
Now double entry – now a flowery trope –
Mingling poetic honey with trade wax –
Blogg, Brothers – Milton – Grote and Prescott – Pope –
Bristles – and Hogg – Glyn Mills and Halifax –
Rogers – and Towgood – Hemp – the Bard of Hope –
Barilla – Byron – Tallow – Burns – and Flax!

Comic Annual, 1833

To My Wife

Still glides the gentle streamlet on,
    With shifting current new and strange
The water, that was here, is gone,
    But those green shadows never change.

Serene or ruffled by the storm,
    On present waves, as on the past,
The mirror'd grove retains its form,
    The self-same trees their semblance cast.

The hue each fleeting globule wears,
    That drop bequeaths it to the next;
One picture still the surface bears,
    To illustrate the murmur'd text.

So, love, however time may flow,
    Fresh hours pursuing those that flee,
One constant image still shall show
    My tide of life is true to thee.

Tylney Hall, 1834

Queen Mab

A little fairy comes at night,
    Her eyes are blue, her hair is brown,
With silver spots upon her wings,
    And from the moon she flutters down.

She has a little silver wand,
    And when a good child goes to bed
She waves her wand from right to left,
    And makes a circle round its head.

And then it dreams of pleasant things,
    Of fountains filled with fairy fish,
And trees that bear delicious fruit,
    And bow their branches at a wish:

Of arbours filled with dainty scents
    From lovely flowers that never fade;
Bright flies that glitter in the sun,
    And glow-worms shining in the shade.

And talking birds with gifted tongues,
    For singing songs and telling tales,
And pretty dwarfs to show the way
    Through fairy hills and fairy dales.

But when a bad child goes to bed,
    From left to right she weaves her rings,
And then it dreams all through the night
    Of only ugly horrid things!

Then lions come with glaring eyes,
    And tigers growl, a dreadful noise,
And ogres draw their cruel knives,
    To shed the blood of girls and boys.

Then stormy waves rush on to drown,
    Or raging flames come scorching round,
Fierce dragons hover in the air,
    And serpents crawl along the ground.

Then wicked children wake and weep,
    And wish the long black gloom away;
But good ones love the dark, and find
    The night as pleasant as the day.

                                    1834 (?)

A Waterloo Ballad

To Waterloo, with sad ado,
    And many a sigh and groan,
Amongst the dead, came Patty Head
    To look for Peter Stone.

'O prithee tell, good sentinel,
    If I shall find him here?
I'm come to weep upon his corse,
    My Ninety-Second dear!

83

'Into our town a serjeant came,
    With ribands all so fine
A-flaunting in his cap – alas!
    His bow enlisted mine!

They taught him how to turn his toes,
    And stand as stiff as starch;
I thought that it was love and May,
    But it was love and March!

A sorry March indeed to leave
    The friends he might have kep', –
No March of Intellect it was,
    But quite a foolish step.

'O prithee tell, good sentinel,
    If hereabout he lies?
I want a corpse with reddish hair,
    And very sweet blue eyes.'

Her sorrow on the sentinel
    Appear'd to deeply strike:
'Walk in,' he said, 'among the dead,
    And pick out which you like.'

And soon she pick'd out Peter Stone,
    Half turned into a corse;
A cannon was his bolster, and
    His mattrass was a horse.

'O Peter Stone, O Peter Stone,
    Lord, here has been a skrimmage!
What have they done to your poor breast,
    That used to hold my image?

'O Patty Head, O Patty Head,
　　You're come to my last kissing;
Before I'm set in the Gazette
　　As wounded, dead, and missing.

'Alas! a splinter of a shell
　　Right in my stomach sticks;
French mortars don't agree so well
　　With stomachs as French bricks.

'This very night a merry dance
　　At Brussels was to be; –
Instead of opening a ball,
　　A ball has open'd me.

'Its billet every bullet has,
　　And well does it fulfil it; –
I wish mine hadn't come so straight,
　　But been a "crooked billet".

'And then there came a cuirassier
　　And cut me on the chest; –
He had no pity in his heart,
　　For he had *steel'd his breast*.

'Next thing a lancer, with his lance
　　Began to thrust away;
I call'd for quarter, but, alas!
　　It was not Quarter-day.

'He ran his spear right through my arm,
　　Just here above the joint: –
O Patty dear, it was no joke,
　　Although it had a point.

'With loss of blood I fainted off
  As dead as women do –
But soon by charging over me,
  The *Coldstreams* brought me to.

'With kicks and cuts, and balls and blows,
  I throb and ache all over;
I'm quite convinced the field of Mars
  Is not a field of clover!

'O why did I a soldier turn,
  For any royal Guelph?
I might have been a butcher, and
  In business for myself!

'O why did I the bounty take?
  (And here he gasped for breath)
My shillingsworth of 'list is nail'd
  Upon the door of death.

'Without a coffin I shall lie,
  And sleep my sleep eternal:
Not ev'n a *shell* – my only chance
  Of being made a *Kernel*!

'O Patty dear, our wedding bells,
  Will never ring at Chester!
Here I must lie in Honour's bed,
  That isn't worth a *tester*!

'Farewell, my regimental mates,
  With whom I used to dress!
My corps is changed, so I am now,
  In quite another mess.

'Farewell, my Patty dear, I have
　　No dying consolations,
Except, when I am dead, you'll go
　　And see th'Illuminations.'
　　　　　　　　　Comic Annual, 1834

Stanzas

Is there a bitter pang for love removed,
　　Oh God! The dead love doth not cost more tears
Than the alive, the loving, the beloved –
　　Not yet, not yet beyond all hopes and fears!
　　　　　Would I were laid
　　　　　Under the shade
Of the calm grave, and the long grass of years, –

That love might die with sorrow: – I am sorrow;
　　And she, that loves me tenderest, doth press
Most poison from my cruel lips, and borrow
　　Only new anguish from the old caress;
　　　　　Oh, this world's grief,
　　　　　Hath no relief,
In being wrung from a great happiness.

Would I had never filled thine eyes with love,
　　For love is only tears: would I had never
Breathed such a curse-like blessing as we prove;
　　Now, if 'Farewell' *could* bless thee, I would sever!
　　　　　Would I were laid
　　　　　Under the shade
Of the cold tomb, and the long grass for ever!
　　　　　　　　　　　　　　1835

Ode to Rae Wilson, Esq.
lines 13-50

...I'm not a saint.
Not one of those self-constituted saints,
Quacks – not physicians – in the cure of souls,
Censors who sniff out mortal taints,
And call the devil over his own coals –
Those pseudo Privy Councillors of God,
Who write down judgements with a pen hard-nibb'd
  Ushers of Beelzebub's Black Rod
Commending sinners, not to ice thick-ribb'd,
But endless flames, to scorch them up like flax, –
Yet sure of heav'n themselves, as if they cribb'd
Th'impression of St Peter's keys in wax!

Of such a character no single trace
Exists, I know, in my fictitious face;
There wants a certain cast about the eye;
A certain lifting of the nose's tip;
A certain curling of the nether lip,
In scorn of all that is, beneath the sky;
In brief it is an aspect deleterious,
A face decidedly not serious,
A face profane, that would not do at all
To make a face at Exeter Hall, –
That Hall where bigots rant, and cant, and pray,
And laud each other face to face,
Till ev'ry farthing-candle *ray*
Conceives itself a great gas-light of grace!

Well! – be the graceless lineaments confest!
I do enjoy this bounteous beauteous earth;
  And dote upon a jest
'Within the limits of becoming mirth'; –
No solemn sanctimonious face I pull,

Nor think I'm pious when I'm only bilious –
Nor study in my sanctum supercilious
To frame a Sabbath Bill or forge a Bull.
I pray for grace – repent each sinful act –
Peruse, but underneath the rose, my Bible;
And love my neighbour, far too well, in fact,
To call and twit him with a godly tract
That's turn'd by application to a libel.
My heart ferments not with the bigot's leaven,
All creeds I view with toleration thorough,
And have a horror of regarding heaven
   As anybody's rotten borough.

lines 133-154

One place there is – beneath the burial sod
Where all mankind are equalized by death;
Another place there is – the Fane of God,
Where all are equal, who draw living breath; –
Juggle who will *elsewhere* with his own soul,
Playing the Judas with a temporal dole –
He who can come beneath that awful cope,
In the dread presence of a Maker just,
Who metes to ev'ry pinch of human dust
One even measure of immortal hope –
He who can stand within that holy door,
With soul unbow'd by that pure spirit-level,
And frame unequal laws for rich and poor, –
Might sit for Hell and represent the Devil!

Such are the solemn sentiments, O Rae,
In your last Journey-Work, perchance, you ravage,
Seeming, but in more courtly terms, to say
I'm but a heedless, creedless, godless savage;

A very Guy, deserving fire and faggots, –
  A Scoffer, always on the grin,
And sadly given to the mortal sin
Of liking Mawworms less than merry maggots!

The Athenaeum, 1837

Sonnet: on Steam
By an Under-Ostler

I wish I livd a Thowsen year Ago
Wurking for Sober six and Seven milers
And dubble Stages runnen safe and slo
The Orsis cum in Them days to the Bilers
But Now by meens of Powers of Steem forces
A-turning Coches into Smoakey Kettels
The Bilers seam a Cumming to the Orses
And Helps and naggs Will sune be out of Vittels
Poor Bruits I wunder How we bee to Liv
When sutch a change of Orses is our Faits
No nothink need Be sifted in a Siv
May them Blowd ingins all Blow up their Grates
And Theaves of Oslers crib the Coles and Giv
Their blackgard Hannimuls a Feed of Slaits!

Hood's Own, 1839

A Lay of Real Life

Who ruined me ere I was born,
Sold every acre, grass or corn,
And left the next heir all forlorn?
            My Grandfather.

Who said my mother was no nurse,
And physicked me and made me worse,
Till infancy became a curse?
          My Grandmother.

Who left me in my seventh year,
A comfort to my mother dear,
And Mr Pope, the overseer?
          My Father.

Who let me starve, to buy her gin,
Till all my bones came through my skin,
Then called me 'ugly little sin?'
          My Mother.

Who said my mother was a Turk,
And took me home – and made me work,
But managed half my meals to shirk?
          My Aunt.

Who 'of all earthly things' would boast,
'He hated others' brats the most,'
And therefore made me feel my post?
          My Uncle.

Who got in scrapes, an endless score,
And always laid them at my door,
Till many a bitter pang I bore?
          My Cousin.

Who took me home when mother died,
Again with father to reside,
Black shoes, clean knives, run far and wide?
          My Stepmother.

Who marred my stealthy urchin joys,
And when I played cried 'What a noise!' –
Girls always hector over boys –
       My Sister.

Who used to share in what was mine,
Or took it all, did he incline,
'Cause I was eight, and he was nine?
       My Brother.

Who stroked my head, and said 'Good lad,'
And gave me sixpence, 'all he had';
But at the stall the coin was bad?
       My Godfather.

Who, gratis, shared my social glass,
But when misfortune came to pass,
Referr'd me to the pump? Alas!
       My Friend.

Through all this weary world, in brief,
Whoever sympathized with grief,
Or shared my joy – my sole relief?
       Myself.

Hood's Own, 1839

Miss Kilmansegg and Her Precious Leg
A Golden Legend

The long cautionary tale of Miss Kilmansegg and her precious leg
('A leg of Gold – solid gold throughout') appeared in the *New
Monthly* as one of the *Rhymes for the Times and Reasons for the Seasons*.
Publication of parts of this 'serial' poem began in 1840 and con-
tinued until the middle of 1841.

The poem traces Miss Kilmansegg's life history: Her Pedigree; Her
Birth; Her Christening; Her Childhood; Her Education; Her Acci-
dent; Her Precious Leg; Her Fame; Her First Step; Her Fancy Ball;
Her Dream; Her Courtship; Her Marriage; Her Honeymoon; Her
Misery; Her Last Will; Her Death; and draws – Her Moral.

Her Fancy Ball
lines 1001-1224

... 'Tis Curiosity's Benefit Night –
And perchance 'tis the English Second-Sight;
    But whatever it be, so be it –
As the friends and guests of Miss Kilmansegg
Crowd in to look at her Golden Leg,
        As many more
        Mob round the door,
    To see them going to see it!

In they go – in jackets and cloaks,
Plumes and bonnets, turbans and toques,
    As if to a Congress of Nations:
Greeks and Malays, with daggers and dirks,
Spaniards, Jews, Chinese, and Turks,
Some like original foreign works,
    But mostly like bad translations.

In they go, and to work like a pack,
Juan, Moses, and Shacabac,
Tom, and Jerry, and Springheel'd Jack,
    For some of low Fancy are lovers –
Skirting, zigzagging, casting about,
Here and there, and in and out,
With a crush, and a rush, for a full-bodied rout
    Is one of the stiffest of covers.

In they went, and hunted about,
Open-mouthed like chub and trout,
And some with the upper lip thrust out,
    Like that fish for routing a barbel –
While Sir Jacob stood to welcome the crowd,
And rubbed his hands, and smiled aloud,
And bow'd, and bow'd, and bow'd, and bow'd,
    Like a man who is sawing marble.

For Princes were there, and noble Peers;
Dukes descended from Norman spears;
Earls that dated from early years;
    And Lords in vast variety –
Besides the Gentry, both new and old –
For people who stand on legs of gold
    Are sure to stand well with society.

'But where-where-where?' with one accord
Cried Moses and Mufti, Jack and my Lord,
    Wang-fong and Il Bondocani –
When slow, and heavy, and dead as a dump,
They heard a foot begin to stump,
        Thump! lump!
        Lump! thump!
    Like the Spectre in 'Don Giovanni!'

And lo! the Heiress, Miss Kilmansegg,
With her splendid, brilliant, beautiful leg,
   In the garb of a Goddess olden –
Like chaste Diana going to hunt,
With a golden spear – which of course was blunt,
And a tunic loop'd up to a gem in front,
   To show that the Leg was Golden!

Gold! still gold! her Crescent behold,
That should be silver, but would be gold;
   And her robe's auriferous spangles!
Her golden stomacher – how she would melt!
Her golden quiver, and golden belt,
   Where a golden bugle dangles!

And her jewelled Garter? Oh, sin! Oh, shame!
Let Pride and Vanity bear the blame,
That bring such blots on female fame!
   But to be a true recorder,
Besides its thin transparent stuff,
The tunic was looped quite high enough
   To give a glimpse of the Order!

But what have sin or shame to do
With a golden Leg – and a stout one too?
   Away with all Prudery's panics!
That the precious metal, by thick and thin,
Will cover square acres of land or sin,
      Is a fact made plain
      Again and again,
   In Morals as well as Mechanics.

A few, indeed, of her proper sex,
Who seemed to feel her foot on their necks,
And feared their charms would meet with checks
   From so rare and splendid a blazon –

A few cried 'fie!' – and 'forward' – and 'bold!'
And said of the Leg, it might be gold,
    But to them it looked like brazen!

'Twas hard, they hinted, for flesh and blood,
Virtue and Beauty, and all that's good,
    To strike to mere dross their top-gallants –
But what were Beauty, or Virtue, or Worth,
Gentle manners, or gentle birth,
Nay, what the most talented head on earth
    To a Leg worth fifty Talents!

But the men sang quite another hymn
Of glory and praise to the precious Limb –
Age, sordid Age, admir'd the whim,
    And its indecorum pardon'd –
While half of the young – ay, more than half –
Bowed down and worshipped the Golden Calf,
    Like the Jews when their hearts were harden'd.

A Golden Leg! what fancies it fir'd!
What golden wishes and hopes inspir'd!
    To give but a mere abridgment –
What a leg to leg-bail Embarrassment's serf!
What a leg for a Leg to take on the Turf!
    What a leg for a marching regiment!

A Golden Leg! – whatever Love sings,
'Twas worth a bushel of 'Plain Gold Rings,'
    With which the Romantic wheedles.
'Twas worth all the legs in stockings and socks –
'Twas a leg that might be put in the Stocks,
    N.B. – Not the parish beadle's!

And Lady K. nid-nodded her head,
Lapp'd in a turban fancy-bred,
Just like a love-apple, huge and red,
   Some Mussul-womanish mystery;
      But whatever she meant
      To represent,
She talk'd like the Muse of History.

She told how the filial leg was lost;
And then how much the gold one cost,
   With its weight to a Trojan fraction;
And how it took off, and how it put on;
And call'd on Devil, Duke, and Don,
Mahomet, Moses, and Prester John,
   To notice its beautiful action.

And then of the Leg she went in quest;
And led it where the light was best;
And made it lay itself up to rest
   In postures for painters' studies:
It cost more tricks and trouble by half,
Than it takes to exhibit a Six-Legged Calf
   To a boothful of country Cuddies.

Nor yet did the Heiress herself omit
The arts that help to make a hit,
   And preserve a prominent station.
She talk'd and laugh'd far more than her share;
And took part in 'Rich and Rare
Were the gems she wore' – and the gems were there,
   Like a Song with an Illustration.

She even stood up with a Count of France –
To dance – alas! the measures we dance
   When Vanity pays the Piper:
Vanity, Vanity, apt to betray,

And lead all sorts of legs astray, –
Wood, or metal, or human clay, –
    Since Satan first played the Viper!

But first she doff'd her hunting gear,
And favour'd Tom Tug with her golden spear
    To row with down the river –
A Bonze had her golden bow to hold;
A Hermit her belt and bugle of gold;
    And an Abbot her golden quiver.

And then a space was clear'd on the floor,
And she walked the Minuet de la Cour,
With all the pomp of a Pompadour,
    But although she began *andante*,
Conceive the faces of all the Rout,
When she finished off with a whirligig bout,
And the Precious Leg stuck stiffly out
    Like the leg of a *Figuranté*!

So the courtly dance was goldenly done,
And golden opinions, of course, it won
    From all different sorts of people –
Chiming, ding-dong, with flattering phrase,
In one vociferous peal of praise,
Like the peal that rings on Royal days
    From Loyalty's parish-steeple.

And yet, had the leg been one of those
That dance for bread in flesh-coloured hose,
    With Rosina's pastoral bevy,
The jeers it had met, the shouts! the scoff!
The cutting advice to 'take itself off,'
    For sounding but half so heavy.

Had it been a leg like those, perchance,
That teach little girls and boys to dance,
To set, poussette, recede, and advance,
　　With the steps and figures most proper, –
Had it hopp'd for a weekly or quarterly sum,
How little of praise or grist would have come
　　To a mill with such a hopper:

But the Leg was none of those limbs forlorn –
Bartering capers and hops for corn –
That meet with public hisses and scorn,
　　Or the morning journal denounces –
Had it pleas'd to caper from morn till dusk,
There was all the music of 'Money Musk,'
　　In it ponderous bangs and bounces.

But, hark! as slow as the strokes of a pump,
　　　　Lump, thump!
　　　　Thump, lump!
As the Giant of Castle Otranto might stump
　　To a lower room from an upper –
Down she goes with a noisy dint,
For taking the crimson turban's hint,
A noble Lord at the Head of the Mint
　　Is leading the Leg to supper!

But the supper, alas! must rest untold,
With its blaze of light, and its glitter of gold,
　　For to paint that scene of glamour,
It would need the Great Enchanter's charm,
Who waves over Palace, and Cot, and Farm,
An arm like the Goldbeater's Golden Arm
　　That wields a Golden Hammer.

He – only *he* could fitly state
The Massive Service of Golden Plate,
   With the proper phrase and expansion –
The rare selection of *Foreign Wines* –
The *Alps of Ice* and *Mountains of Pines*
The punch in *Oceans* and sugary shrines,
The *Temple of Taste* from *Gunter's Designs* –
In short, all that *Wealth* with *a Feast* combines,
   In a *Splendid Family Mansion*.

Suffice it each mask'd outlandish guest,
Ate and drank of the very best,
   According to critical conners –
And then they pledged the Hostess and Host,
But the Golden Leg was the standing toast,
     And as somebody swore,
     Walk'd off with more
Than its share of the 'Hips!' and honours!

     'Miss Kilmansegg! –
     Full glasses I beg! –
Miss Kilmansegg and her Precious Leg! –'
   And away went the bottle careering!
Wine in bumpers! and shouts in peals!
Till the clown didn't know his head from his heels,
The Mussulman's eyes danced twosome reels,
   And the Quaker was hoarse with cheering!

Her Moral

   Gold! Gold! Gold! Gold!
   Bright and yellow, hard and cold,
   Molten, graven, hammer'd, and roll'd;
   Heavy to get, and light to hold;

Hoarded, barter'd, bought, and sold,
Stolen, borrow'd, squander'd, doled:
Spurn'd by the young, but hugg'd by the old
To the very verge of the churchyard mould;
Price of many a crime untold;
Gold! Gold! Gold! Gold:
Good or bad a thousand fold!
    How widely its agencies vary –
To save – to ruin – to curse – to bless –
As even its minted coins express,
Now stamp'd with the image of Good Queen Bess,
    And now of a Bloody Mary!

New Monthly Magazine, 1840-41

The Turtles
lines 18-40

Down narrow streets and crooked lanes they dived,
    Past many a gusty avenue, through which
    Came yellow fog, and smell of pitch,
From barge, and boat, and dusky wharf derived;
With darker fumes, brought eddying by the draught,
    From loco-smoko-motive craft;
Mingling with scents of butter, cheese, and gammons,
Tea, coffee, sugar, pickles, rosin, wax,
Hides, tallow, Russia-matting, hemp and flax,
Salt-cod, red-herrings, sprats, and kipper'd salmons,
        Nuts, oranges, and lemons,
Each pungent spice, and aromatic gum,
Gas, pepper, soaplees, brandy, gin, and rum;
Alamode-beef and greens – the London soil –
Glue, coal, tobacco, turpentine and oil,
Bark, assafœtida, squills, vitriol, hops,
In short, all whiffs, and sniffs, and puffs, and snuffs,

From metals, minerals, and dyewood stuffs,
Fruits, victual, drink, solidities, or slops –
In flasks, casks, bales, trucks, waggons, taverns, shops,
Boats, lighters, cellars, wharfs, and warehouse-tops,
That, as we walk upon the river's ridge,
    Assault the nose – below the bridge.

New Monthly Magazine, 1842

No!

    No sun – no moon!
    No morn – no noon –
No dawn – no dusk – no proper time of day –
    No sky – no earthly view –
    No distance looking blue –
No road – no street – no 't'other side the way' –
    No end to any Row –
    No indications where the Crescents go –
    No top to any steeple –
No recognitions of familiar people –
    No courtesies for showing 'em! –
    No knowing 'em! –
No travelling at all – no locomotion,
No inkling of the way – no notion –
    'No go' – by land or ocean –
    No mail – no post –
No news from any foreign coast –
No Park – no Ring – no afternoon gentility –
    No company – no nobility –
No warmth, no cheerfulness, no healthful ease,
    No comfortable feel in any member –
No shades, no shine, no butterflies, no bees,
    No fruits, no flowers, no leaves, no birds, —
    November!

New Monthly Magazine, 1842

The Song of The Shirt

With fingers weary and worn,
  With eyelids heavy and red,
A Woman sat, in unwomanly rags,
  Plying her needle and thread –
    Stitch! stitch! stitch!
In poverty, hunger, and dirt,
And still with a voice of dolorous pitch
She sang the 'Song of the Shirt!'

'Work! work! work!
While the cock is crowing aloof!
  And work – work – work,
Till the stars shine through the roof!
It's O! to be a slave
  Along with the barbarous Turk,
Where woman has never a soul to save,
  If this is Christian work!

'Work – work – work
Till the brain begins to swim;
  Work – work – work
Till the eyes are heavy and dim!
Seam, and gusset, and band,
  Band, and gusset, and seam,
Till over the buttons I fall asleep,
  And sew them on in a dream!

'O! Men with Sisters dear!
  O! Men! with Mothers and Wives!
It is not linen you're wearing out,
  But human creatures' lives!
    Stitch – stitch – stitch,
  In poverty, hunger, and dirt,
Sewing at once, with a double thread,
  A Shroud as well as a Shirt.

'But why do I talk of Death?
    That Phantom of grisly bone,
I hardly fear his terrible shape,
    It seems so like my own –
    It seems so like my own,
    Because of the fasts I keep,
Oh! God! that bread should be so dear,
    And flesh and blood so cheap!

'Work – work – work!
    My labour never flags;
And what are its wages? A bed of straw,
    A crust of bread – and rags.
That shatter'd roof, – and this naked floor –
    A table – a broken chair –
And a wall so blank, my shadow I thank
    For sometimes falling there!

'Work – work – work!
From weary chime to chime,
    Work – work – work –
As prisoners work for crime!
    Band, and gusset, and seam,
    Seam, and gusset, and band,
Till the heart is sick, and the brain benumb'd,
    As well as the weary hand.

'Work – work – work,
In the dull December light,
    And work – work – work,
When the weather is warm and bright –
While underneath the eaves
    The brooding swallows cling
As if to show me their sunny backs
    And twit me with the spring.

'Oh! but to breathe the breath
Of the cowslip and primrose sweet –
　　With the sky above my head,
And the grass beneath my feet,
For only one short hour
　　To feel as I used to feel,
Before I knew the woes of want
　　And the walk that costs a meal!

'Oh but for one short hour!
　　A respite however brief!
No blessed leisure for Love or Hope,
　　But only time for Grief!
A little weeping would ease my heart,
　　But in their briny bed
My tears must stop, for every drop
　　Hinders needle and thread!'

Seam, and gusset, and band,
Band, and gusset, and seam,
　　　Work, work, work,
Like the Engine that works by Steam!
A mere machine of iron and wood
　　　That toils for Mammon's sake –
Without a brain to ponder and craze
　　　Or a heart to feel – and break!

With fingers weary and worn,
　　With eyelids heavy and red,
A Woman sat in unwomanly rags,
　　Plying her needle and thread –
　　　Stitch! stitch! stitch!
　　In poverty, hunger, and dirt,
And still with a voice of dolorous pitch,
Would that its tone could reach the Rich! –
　　She sang this 'Song of the Shirt!'

Punch, Christmas 1843

The Haunted House
A Romance

PART III

'Tis hard for human actions to account,
Whether from reason or from impulse only –
But some internal prompting bade me mount
The gloomy stairs and lonely.

Those gloomy stairs, so dark, and damp, and cold,
With odours as from bones and relics carnal,
Deprived of rite, and consecrated mould,
The chapel vault, or charnel.

Those dreary stairs, where with the sounding stress
Of ev'ry step so many echoes blended,
The mind, with dark misgivings, fear'd to guess
How many feet ascended.

The tempest with its spoils had drifted in,
Till each unwholesome stone was darkly spotted,
As thickly as the leopard's dappled skin,
With leaves that rankly rotted.

The air was thick – and in the upper gloom
The bat – or something in its shape – was winging,
And on the wall, as chilly as a tomb,
The Death's Head moth was clinging.

That mystic moth, which, with a sense profound
Of all unholy presence, augurs truly;
And with a grim significance flits round
The taper burning bluely.

Such omens in the place there seem'd to be,
At ev'ry crooked turn, or on the landing,
The straining eyeball was prepared to see
Some Apparition standing.

For over all there hung a cloud of fear,
A sense of mystery the spirit daunted,
And said, as plain as whisper in the ear,
The place is Haunted!

Yet no portentous Shape the sight amaz'd;
Each object plain, and tangible, and valid;
But from their tarnish'd frames dark Figures gaz'd,
And Faces spectre-pallid.

Not merely with the mimic life that lies
Within the compass of Art's simulation;
Their souls were looking thro' their painted eyes
With awful speculation.

On every lip a speechless horror dwelt;
On ev'ry brow the burden of affliction;
The old Ancestral Spirits knew and felt
The House's malediction.

Such earnest woe their features overcast,
They might have stirr'd, or sigh'd, or wept, or spoken;
But, save the hollow moaning of the blast,
The stillness was unbroken.

No other sound or stir of life was there,
Except my steps in solitary clamber,
From flight to flight, from humid stair to stair,
From chamber into chamber.

Deserted rooms of luxury and state,
That old magnificence had richly furnish'd
With pictures, cabinets of ancient date,
And carvings rich and burnish'd.

Rich hangings, storied by the needle's art,
With scripture history or classic fable;
But all had faded, save one ragged part,
Where Cain was slaying Abel.

The silent waste of mildew and the moth
Had marr'd the tissue with a partial ravage;
But undecaying frown'd upon the cloth
Each feature stern and savage.

The sky was pale; the cloud a thing of doubt;
Some hues were fresh, and some decay'd and duller;
But still the BLOODY HAND shone strangely out
With vehemence of colour!

The BLOODY HAND that with a lurid stain
Shone on the dusty floor, a dismal token,
Projected from the casement's painted pane,
Where all beside was broken.

The BLOODY HAND significant of crime,
That glaring on the old heraldic banner,
Has kept its crimson unimpair'd by time,
In such a wondrous manner!

O'er all there hung a shadow of a fear,
A sense of mystery the spirit daunted,
And said, as plain as whisper in the ear,
The place is Haunted!

The Death Watch tick'd behind the panel'd oak,
Inexplicable tremors shook the arras,
And echoes strange and mystical awoke,
The fancy to embarrass.

Prophetic hints that filled the soul with dread,
But thro' one gloomy entrance pointing mostly,
The while some secret inspiration said
That chamber is the Ghostly!

Across the door no gossamer festoon
Swung pendulous – no web – no dusty fringes,
No silky chrysalis or white cocoon
About its nooks and hinges.

The spider shunn'd the interdicted room,
The moth, the beetle, and the fly were banish'd,
And where the sunbeam fell athwart the gloom,
The very midge had vanish'd.

One lonely ray that glanc'd upon a Bed,
As if with awful aim direct and certain,
To show the BLOODY HAND in burning red
Embroider'd on the curtain.

And yet no gory stain was on the quilt –
The pillow in its place had slowly rotted;
The floor alone retain'd the trace of guilt,
Those boards obscurely spotted.

Obscurely spotted to the door, and thence
With mazy doubles to the grated casement –
Oh what a tale they told of fear intense,
Of horror and amazement!

What human creature in the dead of night
Had coursed like hunted hare that cruel distance?
Had sought the door, the window in his flight,
Striving for dear existence?

What shrieking Spirit in that bloody room
Its mortal frame had violently quitted? –
Across the sunbeam, with a sudden gloom,
A ghostly shadow flitted.

Across the sunbeam, and along the wall,
But painted on the air so very dimly,
It hardly veil'd the tapestry at all,
Or portrait frowning grimly.

O'er all there hung the shadow of a fear,
A sense of mystery the spirit daunted,
And said, as plain as whisper in the ear,
The place is Haunted!

Hood's Magazine, 1844

The Workhouse Clock
An Allegory

There's a murmur in the air,
And noise in every street –
The murmur of many tongues,
The noise of numerous feet –
While round the Workhouse door
The Labouring Classes flock,
For why? the Overseer of the Poor
Is setting the Workhouse Clock.

Who does not hear the tramp
Of thousands speeding along
Of either sex and various stamp,
Sickly, crippled, or strong,
Walking, limping, creeping
From court, and alley, and lane,
But all in one direction sweeping
Like rivers that seek the main?

Who does not see them sally
From mill, and garret, and room,
In lane, and court and alley,
From homes in poverty's lowest valley,
Furnished with shuttle and loom –
Poor slaves of Civilization's galley –
And in the roads and footways rally,
As if for the Day of Doom?
Some, of hardly human form,
Stunted, crooked, and crippled by toil;
Dingy with smoke and dust and oil,
And smirch'd besides with vicious soil,
Clustering, mustering, all in a swarm.
Father, mother, and careful child,
Looking as if it had never smiled –
The Sempstress, lean, and weary, and wan,
With only the ghosts of garments on –
The Weaver, her sallow neighbour,
The grim and sooty Artisan;
Every soul – child, woman, or man,
Who lives – or dies – by labour.

Stirr'd by an overwhelming zeal,
And social impulse, a terrible throng!
Leaving shuttle, and needle, and wheel,
Furnace, and grindstone, spindle, and reel,
Thread, and yarn, and iron, and steel –

Yea, rest and the yet untasted meal –
Gushing, rushing, crushing along,
A very torrent of Man!
Urged by the sighs of sorrow and wrong,
Grown at last to a hurricane strong,
Stop its course who can!
Stop who can its onward course
And irresistible moral force;
O! vain and idle dream!
For surely as men are all akin,
Whether of fair or sable skin,
According to Nature's scheme,
That Human Movement contains within
A Blood-Power stronger than Steam.

Onward, onward, with hasty feet,
They swarm – and westward still –
Masses born to drink and eat,
But starving amidst Whitechapel's meat,
And famishing down Cornhill!
Through the Poultry – but still unfed –
Christian charity, hang your head!
Hungry – passing the Street of Bread;
Thirsty – the street of Milk;
Ragged – beside the Ludgate Mart,
So gorgeous, through Mechanic-Art,
With cotton, and wool, and silk!

At last, before that door
That bears so many a knock
Ere ever it opens to Sick or Poor,
Like sheep they huddle and flock –
And would that all the Good and Wise
Could see the million of hollow eyes,
With a gleam deriv'd from Hope and the skies,
Upturn'd to the Workhouse Clock!

112

Oh! that the Parish Powers,
Who regulate Labour's hours,
The daily amount of human trial,
Weariness, pain, and self-denial,
Would turn from the artificial dial
That striketh ten or eleven,
And go, for once, by that older one
That stands in the light of Nature's sun,
And takes its time from Heaven!

Hood's Magazine, 1844

The Bridge of Sighs

One more Unfortunate,
Weary of breath,
Rashly importunate,
Gone to her death!

Take her up tenderly,
Lift her with care;
Fashion'd so slenderly,
Young, and so fair!

Look at her garments
Clinging like cerements;
Whilst the wave constantly
Drips from her clothing;
Take her up instantly,
Loving, not loathing. –

Touch her not scornfully;
Think of her mournfully,
Gently and humanly;

113

Not of the stains of her,
All that remains of her
Now is pure womanly.

Make no deep scrutiny
Into her mutiny
Rash and undutiful:
Past all dishonour
Death has left on her
Only the beautiful.

Still, for all slips of hers,
One of Eve's family –
Wipe those poor lips of hers
Oozing so clammily.

Loop up her tresses
Escaped from the comb,
Her fair auburn tresses;
Whilst wonderment guesses
Where was her home?

Who was her father?
Who was her mother?
Had she a sister?
Had she a brother?
Or was there a dearer one
Still, and a nearer one
Yet, than all other?

Alas! for the rarity
Of Christian charity
Under the sun!
Oh! it was pitiful!
Near a whole city full,
Home had she none!

Sisterly, brotherly,
Fatherly, motherly,
Feelings had changed:
Love, by harsh evidence,
Thrown from its eminence;
Even God's providence
Seeming estranged.

Where the lamps quiver
So far in the river,
With many a light
From window and casement,
From garret to basement,
She stood, with amazement,
Houseless by night.

The bleak wind of March
Made her tremble and shiver;
But not the dark arch,
Or the black flowing river:
Mad from life's history,
Glad to death's mystery,
Swift to be hurl'd –
Anywhere, anywhere,
Out of the world!

In she plunged boldly,
No matter how coldly
The rough river ran, –
Over the brink of it,
Picture it – think of it,
Dissolute man!
Lave in it, drink of it,
Then, if you can!

Take her up tenderly,
Lift her with care;
Fashion'd so slenderly,
Young, and so fair!

Ere her limbs frigidly
Stiffen too rigidly,
Decently, – kindly, –
Smoothe and compose them:
And her eyes, close them,
Staring so blindly!

Dreadfully staring
Thro' muddy impurity,
As when with the daring
Last look of despairing,
Fix'd on futurity.

Perishing gloomily,
Spurr'd by contumely,
Cold inhumanity,
Burning insanity,
Into her rest. –
Cross her hands humbly,
As if praying dumbly,
Over her breast!

Owning her weakness,
Her evil behaviour,
And leaving, with meekness,
Her sins to her Saviour!

Hood's Magazine, 1844

Epigrams

On The Arrangement of The Statues in Trafalgar Square

If Nelson looks down on a couple of Kings,
    However it pleases the Loyals;
Tis after the fashion of nautical things,
    A Sky-scraper over the Royals.

Hood's Magazine, 1844

The Superiority of Machinery

A Mechanic his labour will often discard,
    If the rate of his pay he dislikes;
But a clock – and its *case* is uncommonly hard –
    Will continue to work, though it *strikes*!

Whimsicalities, 1844

When would-be Suicides in purpose fail –
Who could not find a morsel though they needed –
If Peter sends them for attempts to jail,
What would he do to them if they succeeded?

Hood's Magazine, 1844

My heart's wound up just like a watch,
    As far as springs will take –
It wants but one more evil turn,
    And then the cords will break!

1845

Stanzas

Farewell, Life! My senses swim:
And the world is growing dim;
Thronging shadows cloud the light,
Like the advent of the night, –
Colder, colder, colder still
Upward steals a vapour chill –
Strong the earthy odour grows –
I smell the Mould above the Rose!

Welcome, Life! the Spirit strives!
Strength returns, and hope revives;
Cloudy fears and shapes forlorn
Fly like shadows of the morn, –
O'er the earth there comes a bloom –
Sunny light for sullen gloom,
Warm perfume for vapour cold –
I smell the Rose above the Mould!

Hood's Magazine, 1845

Notes

INTRODUCTION

7 *'While in Germany...'* Extract from *Memorials of Thomas Hood*, F.F. Broderip (Hood's daughter), 1860. A note by his son, Tom Hood, to a letter from Jane Hood to Mrs Elliot, 29 Oct. 1836.

Paul and Virginia from the French *Paul et Virginie* by Bernadin de St Pierre, which Hood claimed to have translated; the translation has not been traced.

'practicable' a theatrical term, indicating parts of the scenery capable of actual use in the play.

8 *as an engraver* Hood appears to have worked as a free lance, executing topographical work for one of the le Keux brothers.

'Perhaps you will ask...' Letter to George Rollo, October 1821, *Memorials*, op.cit. *The Letters of Thomas Hood* have been edited by Peter F. Morgan, Edinburgh, 1973.

'that half-Hogarth...' Lamb's review was for *The New Monthly Magazine*, XVI, February 1826. The cartoon, in The British Museum, is reproduced in John Clubbe, *Victorian Forerunner*, Duke University Press, 1968.

9 *The London Magazine* was founded in 1820 in opposition to Blackwood's; it was bought by Taylor and Hessey in 1821 on the death in a duel of its first editor, John Scott.

'I dreamt articles...' from *Literary Reminiscences*, printed in *Hood's Own*, 1839.

10 *'In outward appearance...'* A recollection in *Pen and Pencil* by Mrs Balmanno, New York, 1858; quoted in the *Memorials*, op.cit.

'Methodist face' Letter to Philip de Franck, January 1838, *Letters*, ed. Morgan, p348.

The Literary Fund *The Royal Literary Fund* was established in 1790 for the relief of authors in financial difficulties.

'What a fertile genius...' in a letter to Bernard Barton, *Letters of Charles Lamb*, ed. E.V. Lucas, London, 1935.

119

He ... was a man of great power writing to Angela Burdett-Coutts, March 1845.

11 *'an age of literary industry'* Prospectus to *Hood's Own*, Jan. 1838

Hood died in 1845 ... he was buried in Kensal Green Cemetery. Some time after his death, a monument, paid for by public subscription, was raised over the grave. It remains – but the bust of the poet and the decorative panels illustrating his poems are missing.

the Athenaeum a literary review founded in 1828; it was at its most successful when owned and edited by Hood's friend, Charles Wentworth Dilke. Hood continued to write for it after ending his financial involvement.

12 *He writes for bread* Letter to *The Athenaeum*, Hood *Works*, 1862, Vol VI, p.114.

13 *Krak kraziboo ban* from 'A Flying Visit', *Comic Annual*, 1839.

Auden's admiration 'When Hood (whom *I*, by the way, consider a major poet) ... is writing as a comic poet, he is like nobody but himself and serious in the true sense of the word.' *Introduction to Nineteenth Century British Minor Poets*, 1966, p.17.

14 *To make laugh is my calling* quoted from the *Memorials* by Thackeray in *Roundabout Papers*, 'On a Joke I once heard from the Late Thomas Hood'.

Grimaldi See note on page 122 below.

to shoot folly as it flies Preface, *Comic Annual*, 1834.

15 *Porteous* leader of the Porteous riots of 1736, described by Scott in *The Heart of Midlothian*.

cannon Hood's miniature cannon may have suggested this detail in Dickens's description of Wemmick's 'castle' in *Great Expectations*.

Tom Pinch Letter to Dickens, 4 December 1843. *Letters*, ed. Morgan, p.577.

17 *'The Elm Tree'* is not included in this selection. As in 'The Haunted House' Hood builds up an atmosphere of foreboding as the speaker voices his premonition that a particular elm will furnish the timber for his coffin.

18 *Hartley Coleridge* letter to Hood, 1831 quoted by Tom Hood, *Works*, 1862, Vol I, p.86 n.

20 *Ode to Rae Wilson* published in *The Athenaeum*, 12 August 1837. Rae Wilson (1772-1849), a Scot of narrow Protestant views, repeatedly attacked Hood for irreligion, from the publication of Hood's etching *The Progress of Cant* onwards.

New Monthly Magazine founded in 1814, took the place of *The London Magazine* when this declined. Hood was an occasional contributor and became editor in 1841 on the death of Theodore Hook.

21 *'The Lay of the Labourer'* in *Hood's Magazine*, November 1844 was a plea, largely in prose, on behalf of the agricultural labourer. It contained a 'lay' with the refrain 'A spade! a rake! a hoe! and the message:

> 'Ay, only give me work,
>   And then you need not fear
> That I shall snare his worship's hare,
>   Or kill his grace's deer;'

22 *'domestic poetry'* Preface, *Comic Annual*, 1837

23 *the dignity of the craft* from Hood's first letter to *The Athenaeum*, 1837, on the subject of *Copyright and Copywrong*.

24 *'wealth of the claims of want...'* from Hood's review of *The Chimes*, *Hood's Magazine*, 1845.

'his drift...' Letter to C.W. Dilke, November 1839. *Letters*, ed. Morgan, p.396.

Here is a man... see note to p.14.

THE POEMS

27 *To Hope* the first poem of Hood's to be published in *The London Magazine*, November, 1821. Cf. his last poem, p.118.

The Sea of Death this fragment was included in Hood's volume *The Plea of The Midsummer Fairies*, 1827; as were all the poems marked † in the Table of Contents.

29 *Faithless Sally Brown*
eye-water eye lotion; it became a slang term for gin.
old Benbow John Benbow (1653-1702) was a famous admiral.
tender a small boat used to ferry people and goods to a larger vessel.
to pipe his eye in nautical slang 'to weep'.

31 *Lycus, the Centaur*
Circe, the sorceress, turned the companions of Ulysses into swine.

35 *To Fancy guest* the early version has 'quest'.

36 *Fair Ines* the third stanza was added later.

42 *The Forsaken* Tom Hood, on the evidence of his father's commonplace book, dates this 1824.

Odes and Addresses to Great People

45 *Ode to Mr Graham* Mr Graham made a celebrated balloon ascent in 1823.
the Eagle presumably the public house in the City Rd celebrated in 'Pop goes the Weasel'.
the Dolland the telescope – known by its maker's name.
Mogg's probably Edward Moggs who published topographical works including *A Pocket Itinerary of the Roads of England and Wales*.
Mac Adamized another of the Odes (by Reynolds) is addressed to John L. MacAdam (1756-1836) whose road-surfacing method was introduced about 1820.
Gogs a reference to the carved wooden figures of the giants Gog and Magog in the Guildhall, London.
another brace of bags of the sand used for ballast.
Dukes of Gloster Hood frequently makes puns involving 'Double' and 'Single' Gloucester cheeses.

48 *A Friendly Address to Mrs Fry* in *Newgate* originally *A Friendly Epistle...* to Elizabeth Fry, the Quaker prison-reformer (1780-1845).

Miss Nancy Dawson Most of the names Hood uses for the women of Newgate are taken from Gay's *Beggar's Opera*. Nancy Dawson (1730?-67), however, was a dancer famous for performances of the hornpipe in productions of the play at both Covent Garden and Drury Lane. She was notoriously immoral and the subject of a popular 'Ballad of Nancy Dawson' sung to the hornpipe tune – better known today as 'Here we go round the Mulberry Bush'. 'Long Sal' has not been traced.

Pandeans bands made up of players on the pan-pipes.

Newgatory Coleridge declared the pun 'transcendant'.

Porch an allusion to the Stoics.

Mr Wontner John Wontner (1784-1833) became Governor of Newgate in 1822 after he sustained extensive injuries in a riding accident whilst carrying out his duties as Upper Marshall of the City of London; he was in advance of his time as a prison-reformer.

50 *Ode to Joseph Grimaldi* Grimaldi (1779-1837) the famous theatrical clown, credited with creating the familiar costume and make-up of the clown (or 'Joe'); Hood wrote Grimaldi's Farewell Address for his last appearance, in 1828. The Ode, given here in its entirety, was Lamb's favourite among the *Odes and Addresses*: 'I liked Grimaldi best: it is true painting of abstract clownery, and that precious concrete of a Clown.' Letter to Coleridge, 2 June 1827.

Young of *Night Thoughts*.

Pantaloon a traditional character in 16th century Italian comedy; a foolish old man – the butt of the clown's jokes.

reverend Croly George Croly (1780-1860) rector of St Stephen's, Walbrook, wrote romances and *Catiline*, a tragedy – Byron's 'Revd Rowley Powley' *Don Juan*, xi.57.

Robert Southey (1774-1843) Poet Laureate.

Mr Fletcher Probably Alexander Fletcher (1787-1860), a popular presbyterian preacher suspended from office in 1824 after involvement in a breach of promise case. He published appeals against his suspension and other works, including *The Loves of the Saints*, 1825. Hood shows a copy of Fletcher's 'Appeal' being trampled underfoot in his engraving *The Progress of Cant*.

Poole John Poole (1786?-1872) author of successful farces such as *Paul Pry, Lodgings for Single Gentlemen*.

Dibdin Charles Dibdin (1745-1814) actor, dramatist and song-writer (author of 'Tom Bowling'); his two sons, Charles (1768-1833) and Tom (1771-1841) were active at Covent Garden, Drury Lane and Sadler's Wells; they were responsible for many of the most famous pantomimes of the time, in which Grimaldi was the principal attraction; a nephew also wrote for the stage.

Byewaye Highway Man Thomas Colley Gratton (1792-1864) author of *Highways and Byways*, 1823.

Skeffy Sir Lumley Skeffington (1771-1850) wrote *The Sleeping Beauty* and was responsible for stage productions renowned for their scenic effects.

Kirby James Kirby was one of Grimaldi's successors as a clown and *Signor Paulo* (1787-1835) the best known of his successors at the Wells.

Joseph Wilfred Parkins was Sheriff of London in the 1820s; Hood mentions him in the 'Ode to W Kitchener, M.D.' as frequenting the Conversazioni which the Doctor held in Warren St.

Waithman Robert Waithman (1764-1833) was Lord Mayor in 1823; he took an interest in the arts and belonged to some of the literary societies of the time.

Cobbett an allusion to the fact-finding journeys he made in the 1820s; his findings were collected in *Rural Rides* in 1830.

Bowles Revd William Lisle Bowles (1762-1850) remembered for *Fourteen Sonnets*; he edited Pope's works. Byron called him 'the maudlin prince of mournful sonneteers'.

Medwin Thomas Medwin (1788-1869) biographer of Shelley, produced his controversial *Journal of the Conversations of Lord Byron* in 1824 shortly after Byron's death.

Irving probably the charismatic preacher Edward Irving (1792-1834) who, as Hazlitt's description of him in *The Spirit of the Age* stresses, was exceptionally tall – rather than Washington Irving, although he was writing in England at this time and known to Hood.

Lady Morgan (1783?-1859) largely famous for a romance of Irish life *The Wild Irish Girl*.

Berkeley's Foote Maria Foote (1797-1867) was a celebrated actress of the time; beautiful rather than talented, she had a succession of scandalous love affairs, including a long-standing relationship with Colonel Berkeley; she retired from the stage in 1831 to marry the Earl of Harrington.

Winter Thomas Winter (1795-1851) a famous pugilist, was known in the ring as Tom Spring.

Munden Joseph S. Munden (1758-1832) was 'One of the Old Actors', a comedian on the legitimate stage; Lamb has left a number of descriptions of his performances, including that of *Dozey*. Mary Lamb has been credited with the pun on Munden's name. *Liston* also was among the comedians of the time. *Charles Farley* was associated with Covent Garden from childhood and was a producer of the pantomimes.

Kemble John Philip Kemble (1757-1823) famous for tragic roles. Mr Willet and Captain John Forbes R.N. were associated with Kemble in a dispute among the proprietors of Covent Garden. The matter was eventually settled when Kemble, Forbes and Willet leased the theatre from Henry Harris who held the majority shareholding. There is, therefore, a pun on 'reign'.

Quick John Quick (1748-1831) another of the old Covent Garden comic actors.

Ghost of Grimm *Grimm's Ghost* was the title of a long-running series of 'Letters' in imitation of the *Correspondences Littéraires* of Baron Grimm; the author was James Smith (1775-1839).

Joe Frankenstein one of Grimaldi's famous acts was to construct a man entirely of vegetables; the 'medley coach' was made of pots and pans.

Joseph Junior (1802-1832) followed his father's calling for a short time, but pre-deceased him.

54 *An Address to the Steam Washing Company*

Allan-a-dale a minstrel in the Robin Hood ballads; appears also in Scott's *Ivanhoe*.

copper refers to the vessel in which the linen was boiled; *alkaline broth* to lye and *pearl ashes* to potassium carbonate – both used as bleaching agents.

Sir Astley Cooper the famous surgeon (1768-1841).

55 *The Water Lady* According to Tom Hood the lines were inspired by a little water-colour sketch of a nymph, by Severn, given to his mother Jane (Reynolds) by Keats: the poem, therefore, has a direct, as well as an obvious stylistic link with Keats.

56 *The Last Man* cp. Byron *Darkness* (1816); Campbell *The Last Man* (1823); Mary Shelley *The Last Man* (1826).

orts scraps of left-over food. *Newgate-bird* jailbird

mumping begging

corals given to babies to bite on when teething

blinded blindfolded; the allusion is to the practice of allowing the friends of the hanged man to shorten his suffering by pulling his legs.

64 *I remember, I remember,* probably a reminiscence of the Islington house in which Hood spent his boyhood, rather than of the house in The Poultry, where he was born.

65 *[In Memoriam]* the lines, with a curl of hair, were found among Hood's papers after his death. The death of the Hoods' first child was also commemorated in Lamb's lines *On an Infant Dying as soon as born*.

66 *Bianca's Dream* Hood read an early version of the poem to the North London Literary Society, of which he was a member, in 1820.

'winsome marrow' from *The Braes of Yarrow*, by William Hamilton (1704-1754); 'marrow' = mate, companion.

Glassite a sect founded by Revd John Glas (1695-1773), expelled from the established Church of Scotland for maintaining that national churches are unlawful.

Gloster   see note p.122.

telegraphs   probably refers to a semaphore signalling device which used an arrangement of movable wooden arms; invented in France by Chappe, 1793.

Be thou my park   Shakespeare, *Venus and Adonis*, line 231, 'I'll be a park, and thou shalt be my deer.'

sparks   her 'beaux'.

71   *On Mistress Nicely*   In the *Literary Magnet* this appeared as *Sonnet on The Mistress Cicely, a Pattern and Example for Housekeepers* and may have been printed elsewhere before this. Mrs Davenport (1765-1843) was a well-known actress. The character is from *The School of Reform* by Thomas Morton.

73   *The Dream of Eugene Aram*   first published in *The Gem* 1829; it was then published separately in 1831 with wood engravings by Wm. Harvey. Admiral Burney (the brother of Fanny Burney) recalled that Aram, who was Usher at the school he attended in Kings Lynn, would talk to his pupils about murder in something of the manner described in the poem.

The Death of Abel   an anachronism – the popular English translation of Gessner's *Der Tod Abels* (1758) appeared sixteen years after the murder in 1745 for which Aram was arrested fourteen years later.

80   *The Death Bed*   the poem may recall the death of Hood's mother or possibly that of his sister Anne, but the date of her death remains uncertain. Tom Hood records that his father had no copy of the verses but that Mary Lamb had saved a newspaper cutting of them in a scrap book; he dates the poem 1825 – it was republished in *The Englishman's Magazine* for 1831.

81   *Sonnet: Time was I sat upon a lofty stool*   This autobiographical sonnet was reprinted at the front of Hood's *Literary Reminiscences* in *Hood's Own*, 1839; the firm for which he worked has not been identified.

Castalian pool   a fountain of Parnassus, sacred to the Muses.

The Bard of Hope Thomas Campbell, who wrote *The Pleasures of Hope*, 1799.

barilla   a Spanish plant, like hemp and flax, used in wick-making.

To my Wife   although published in the novel *Tylney Hall* these lines have traditionally been held to be addressed to Jane Hood – as, according to Tom Hood, were all originals of love poems in his possession – he dates them 1825.

82   *Queen Mab*   the date is uncertain; Tom Hood guesses 1834.

83   *A Waterloo Ballad*   republished in *Hood's Own*, which, issued in monthly parts in 1839 contained verse and prose, most of which had been previously published between 1830 and 1838 in Hood's *Comic Annual*.

Ninety-Second   the ninety-second Regiment of Foot (Gordon Highlanders) served at Waterloo.

the Gazette   *The London Gazette*, which listed 'wounded, dead, and missing.'

bricks   loaves (briques de pain)

Every bullet has its billet   or 'has a name on it'.

crooked billet   a play on the twin meanings of 'commandeered lodgings' and the name given to the piece of timber which results when a crooked branch is split with wedges along the grain.

steel'd his breast   a reference to the steel breastplates worn by the cuirassiers.

Quarter-day   pay-day

Coldstream   the Coldstream Guards, one of five regiment of foot.

Guelph   English kings of the House of Hanover were descended from Guelphs, the mediaeval Italian political party.

butcher   probably a glance at General Blucher the Prussian general at Waterloo.

My shillingsworth of 'list   the new recruit's acceptance of a shilling legally bound him to the army.

tester   a canopied bed; also a sixpence.

Illuminations   at the victory celebrations.

88   *Ode to Rae Wilson, Esq.*   see Introduction, p.20 and note.

Exeter Hall opened in 1831, was the centre of Evangelical Puritanism.

'within the limits...' *Love's Labour's Lost*, II i.

mawworms Mawworm was a character in Bickerstaffe's play, *The Hypocrite* (1769), a pretender to sanctity.

maggot a whimsical person

90 *Sonnet: on Steam* Hood wrote a number of pieces in both prose and verse on the impact of the coming of steam.

slaits poor quality, slaty, coal.

93 *Miss Kilmansegg and her Precious Leg* was published as one of the *Rhymes for the Times* between 1840 and 1841. Its topicality would not have been lost on the public: Queen Victoria married Prince Albert in 1840. The number of Hanoverian families resident in London was decreasing but a family with a name similar to the unlikely sounding 'Kilmansegg' had been resident there not long before the poem was written.

In they go the device of the Fancy dress ball allows all the world and all sorts and conditions to be present.

Shacabac a beggar in *The Arabian Nights*, tempted by many illusory banquets, he finally attended a real one.

Tom and Jerry and Spring-heel'd Jack characters from Pierce Egan's *Life in London, 1821*.

Mufti a Mohammedan priest

Wang Fong, The Clown of China, Charles Dibdin's pantomime of 1812; *Il Bondocani, or the Caliph Robber*, Thomas Dibdin's Covent Garden pantomime of 1800.

strike their top-gallants a play on the sailors' words for lowering the top sail on the tallest mast: a signal of defeat.

leg-bail to abscond or make a get-away

Plain gold rings presumably a popular ballad of the time.

Muse of History Clio; that is to say, prosaically.

Trojan fraction Troy weight is used for precious metals.

Prester John the legendary Christian King and priest, said to have ruled in Asia.

Cuddies simpletons (a Northern name for a donkey)

'Rich and rare...'   a popular ballad by Thomas Moore.

Tom Tug   the honest but foolish young waterman in Dibdin's *The Waterman*, 1774.

a Bonze   a Buddhist

Figuranté   non-speaking actor/actress or ballet-dancer

Rosina's...   a troupe of rustic dancers

poussette   to dance with joined hands

Money Musk   a country dance tune

Giant...   in Horace Walpole's *Castle of Otranto*, 1764.

Great Enchanter   the name given to a famous auctioneer, George Henry Robins (1778-1847).

Goldbeaters' Golden Arm   probably an allusion to the trade sign traditionally displayed outside the Goldbeaters' shop.

Gunter's Designs   Gunter's was a confectioners in Berkeley Square. Gunter's *Confectioner's Oracle*, containing recipes for desserts, was published in 1830.

conners   inspectors (or 'connoisseurs'?)

101   *The Turtles*

assafoetida   a solidified resinous gum, smelling strongly of garlic, used in cookery and medicine.

squills   a type of lily bulb, used in medicine as a purgative.

103   *The Song of the Shirt*   *The Times* of 26 October 1843 had carried a police report of a woman who attempted to support herself and her two children by sewing trousers at 7d a pair; in order to buy food she pawned some of the material entrusted to her and was unable to redeem it. She was charged with theft and the case gave rise to leaders, articles and correspondence. Hood's poem appeared in *Punch*, 16 December 1843.

110   *The Workhouse Clock*   The Poor Law of 1834 established workhouses which employed both 'indoor' and 'outdoor' poor. The 'clock' was set every morning by the 'Overseer of the Poor' to indicate the beginning of the working day for those claiming benefits.

113   *The Bridge of Sighs*   Hood wrote the poem to commemorate the many suicides who fell to their deaths from Waterloo Bridge, but the impetus for it probably came from the case of Mary Furley who attempted to drown herself and her youngest child in the Regent's Park Canal. The child died and Furley was sentenced to death; there was an outcry in *The Times* in March and April 1844 and the sentence of execution was commuted to deportation for seven years. The poem was translated by Baudelaire in his *Petits Poèmes en Prose*.

117 *Epigrams*
'*When would be suicides...*'   suicide was a criminal offence until 1961.

118 *Stanzas*   reputedly the last poem Hood wrote.

Index of first lines